TOO DEEP FOR WORDS

P9-EGL-968

Rediscovering Lectio Divina

Thelma Hall, R.C.

With 500 Scripture Texts for Prayer

PAULIST PRESS
NEW YORK / MAHWAH

Book design by Nighthawk Design.

Library of Congress Cataloging-in-Publication Data

Hall, Thelma.
    Too deep for words: rediscovering Lectio Divina / Thelma Hall;
  with 500 Scripture texts for prayer.
        p.   cm.
    Bibliography: p.
    ISBN 0-8091-2959-0 (pbk.): $6.95 (est.)
    1. Spiritual life—Catholic authors.   2. Contemplation.   3. Bible—
Devotional use.   I. Title.   II. Title: Lectio Divina.
BX2350.2.H34 1988   87-30708
248.3—dc19   CIP

Published by Paulist Press
997 Macarthur Boulevard
Mahwah, New Jersey 07430

Printed and bound in the
United States of America

Contents

Acknowledgements

A sequence of people helped to bring this book out of fantasy into reality, and I want to thank them.

I had talked often about hoping to "some day" publish a collection of Scripture Themes, with an introductory chapter on how to use Scripture for prayer. That was the fantasy.

When two mutual friends, Sr. Jane Reilly and Bob Hamma, met in Hondo Valle, a tiny village in the Dominican Republic, a year or so ago, and Bob mentioned that part of his work as an editor at Paulist Press was to find new authors, Jane replied, "Why don't you talk to Thelma?" That was the beginning of the reality.

Kathleen O'Brien, the other half of our community in the Cenacle Retreat House in Bedford Village, N.Y.—where we two carry out our ministry of providing directed retreats and ongoing spiritual direction—gave the unconditional support and encouragement without which it would have been impossible for me to complete this book. It took thirteen weeks of "part time" away from Bedford, between October 1986 and April 1987. During those weeks Kathleen carried on alone all the functions of a busy retreat house, in addition to her own part-time work outside, and always with enthusiasm and a smile!

Lou McWhirter graciously provided the ideal "hermitage" apartment for my work, at her home in Yaphank, N.Y., and Mike Boyd's kindness and generosity in making available computer/word processor equipment put the final pieces in place. Meanwhile, the original idea of a single introductory chapter on using Scripture for prayer grew into the present book.

I also want to express my appreciation to my Cenacle religious community, which over the many years since my entrance has helped to form and nurture the substance of this writing.

Gratitude is due too to all those whose interest and promised prayer have been a tangible support to me in this venture. Finally, my thanks to editor Bob Hamma for his original invitation and all his patient guidance of this "new author."

Introduction

Recent years have witnessed a proliferation of methods and techniques of prayer—we have books and articles, conferences and workshops, tapes and videos, in endless profusion; they instruct us in the prayer of the body, the prayer of the imagination, the prayer of the memory, of the senses, of imagery, of healing, etc., etc. Perhaps this is a matter of "supply and demand" and a positive sign of the growing desire for the transcendent, for meaning in life in an increasingly frantic and nuclear-haunted world—that is, for God. Certainly it is a desire which he seems to have implanted in the hearts of countless people today. It is his gift, and the pledge of his desire for us. As we find in the Letter of James: "The longing of the spirit (God) sent to dwell in us is a jealous longing" (Jas 4:5).

It appears to be creating in the Christian community at large a Spirit-awakened hunger for deeper prayer, together with a marked resurgence of interest in contemplative prayer and its practice. It seems timely therefore to offer a book specifically designed to encourage and implement a rediscovery of an ancient Christian way of prayer known as Lectio Divina, which has contemplation as its assumed culmination.

Despite many centuries of fruitful practice, Lectio Divina, with its inherent opening to contemplation, gradually fell into disuse (except in monastic practice) toward the end of the Middle Ages. In place of this spontaneous and uncomplicated way of prayer, systematized categories of "mental prayer," divided into separate methods and forms, were taught. By the end of the sixteenth century contemplation had been relegated to a category not for "ordinary" people, was held in suspicion, and was explicitly discouraged as dangerously bordering on heresy.

Eventually it came to be generally accepted that contemplation was an extraordinary grace, restricted to an elite few. This was in total contradiction to the traditional teaching of the first fifteen centuries that contemplation is open to all Christians as the normal development of an authentic spiritual life.

To further clear away the cloud of misconceptions which have gathered around it over recent centuries, it should be added that contemplative prayer is not a rare reward for excellence or virtue— nor is it a "spiritual high" to be pursued for our own gratification, much less a singular mark of God's special love or approval. Neither is it a luxury of some rarefied "spiritual life." It is an effect of being literally "in love" with God, at the deepest level of the relationship with him for which we are created.

We have been taught as Christians, and presumably have believed, that "we are created for union with God"—but in practice we seem not to dare to accept the full implications of this on a subjective level, to really embrace it as the central truth of our lives. Least of all, perhaps, are we prepared to trust that this is God's passionate desire for us. (How frustrating, for the Lover!)

At best, perhaps we vaguely accept that somehow, somewhere, "in heaven," we will come to this union of love. But Jesus' life and teachings concern our lives here and now: "The kingdom of heaven is within you" . . . "Repent, and believe the good news": you are beloved of God! His message is that we love him in loving one another, and that that love is the love of God, living and loving through us in this world, as its source, meaning and end.

It is this love which becomes experiential in contemplative prayer, and gradually in-forms our lives to become more and more a presence of God's love in the world. That love is not confined to time and space, and exerts a creative power which is the one true source of hope in a world tempted to hopelessness in the face of threatened extinction. It has been bluntly stated, "If you do not believe that evil will be overcome by good"—(or hatred by love)— "you are an atheist." Nevertheless that "overcoming" will not take its course without us, but through our active engagement with God's love and our surrender to it as the only power that will save his world.

Contemplative prayer is consent to that love. It is not "pie in the sky by-and-by when you die," but part of a lifetime process—often costly and painful—of self-emptying and reorientation to selfless love, i.e., a serious following of Jesus. It is, therefore, vitally important today.

Lectio Divina was a proven path to contemplation for centuries. It is time to rediscover the gift.

PART ONE

The Call to Contemplation

CHAPTER ONE

The Rediscovery of Contemplation

There is an inner dynamic in the evolution of all true love that leads to a level of communication "too deep for words." There the lover becomes inarticulate, falls silent, and the beloved receives the silence as eloquence.

This book is about a simple and time-honored way of prayer which, through a gentle unfolding, opens us to that deep level of communication with the Divine. From earliest times in Christian tradition the way has been known as "Lectio Divina."

Lectio, as I shall refer to it hereafter, is a holistic way of prayer which disposes, opens and "in-forms" us for the gift of contemplation God waits to give, by leading us to a meeting place with him in our deepest center, his life-giving dwelling place. It begins this movement by introducing us to the power of the word of God in scripture to speak to the most intimate depths of our hearts, to gift and challenge and change us, and to promote genuine spiritual growth and maturity.

A Hidden Treasure

Long ago, and for many centuries, Lectio proved its great capacity as an effective instrument of the Holy Spirit in prayer, but today it is a "treasure hidden in a field" of obscurity. This fact has been confirmed within the radius of my personal experience, in the retreat house which is the place of my ministry.

Prior to beginning this book I was curious to learn how many of the religious, clergy and laypeople who come for directed retreats and ongoing spiritual direction had a clear notion of the meaning of Lectio. Only a few of the responses to my queries were even close to the literal meaning—for example, "Doesn't it have something to do with reading the Bible?" None reflected any real knowledge of its significant spiritual role in Christian tradition. Of more practical importance, no one expressed any awareness of its value and potential in our own time for those graced with a desire for a deeper experience of prayer.

I recall my own ignorance of Lectio, when as a recent convert to Catholicism I came upon a reference to it and had no conception of its meaning, or even that it had any connection with prayer. It was not many years after a radically life-changing baptism, when the reality of a religious vocation, unplanned and uninvited, was beginning to invade my subconscious.

At that time I was attending Pratt Institute in Brooklyn as an art student. My daily walk from the Long Island railroad station to school brought me past the "Ave Maria Shop," a small Catholic bookstore. It was run by a charming couple who encouraged my insatiable curiosity concerning the new world of Catholicism. Thomas Merton's books, *The Seven Storey Mountain* and *Seeds of Contemplation,* had already created in me an interest in the contemplative life—which I was not yet ready to fully acknowledge. Perhaps it was because reading about the Trappist life seemed "safe" (obviously I could not be thinking about entering that Order!) that I eagerly read a detailed account of the monks' horarium, one of those days when I "just dropped in."

The "horarium" was the hour-by-hour—or in some instances the minute-by-minute—schedule of the Trappists' daily life at that time, before Vatican II. I remember distinctly how puzzled I was to find only one or two specific periods of time set aside for "meditation." How could this be, I wondered, since these men were the great mystics and contemplatives of the Church (or so I had idealized them, every one!). What I did not associate at all with prayer were the many periods throughout the day which were set aside for what was simply named "reading." It was not until a few years later when I was a religious of the Cenacle, a congregation whose lifestyle at that time was monastic and clearly oriented to a contemplative mode of prayer, that I realized that those hours of time scheduled daily for "reading" referred to the practice of Lectio as an entry to contemplative prayer. It was not the simple "spiritual reading" I had assumed it to be.

I also came to know that Lectio's origins were to be found in the beginnings of monasticism, and that it had a long and living history, reaching back before the sixth century, as attested to in the Rule of St. Benedict. Since the monasteries were in those times the centers of learning and spirituality, lay persons as well as monastics were presented with this way of prayer.

Today, however, while Lectio is still practiced as a unique characteristic of monastic prayer, particularly by monks of the Benedictine-Cistercian (Trappist) tradition, the Christian community as a whole seems to have lost awareness of its existence, and of its value as a formative instrument for the growth of Christ's life within us. This has been a considerable loss, particularly because of its direct relationship to the development of contemplative prayer, which is its ultimate fruition.

A Methodless Method

In explaining the dynamics of Lectio the words "meditation" and "contemplation" will be used frequently. Because in recent years they have often been used ambiguously and even interchangeably, it would be well to clarify at this point how they will be understood in these pages.

The word *meditation* refers to a discursive reasoning process in which words, events, etc., are prayerfully pondered and reflected on with the object of drawing from them some personal meaning or moral. It is basically an activity of the intellect and reason, aided by grace.

Contemplation is variously described as a "resting" in God, or a "loving gaze" upon him, or a "knowing beyond knowing," or a "rapt attention" to God. All such attempts at verbalizing the experience necessarily fail to express the reality, for the simple reason that contemplation transcends the thinking and reasoning of meditation, as well as the emotions and "feelings" of the affective faculties. It is basically a prayer and experience of pure faith.[1]

Lectio has sometimes been called a "methodless method" of prayer. The description alludes to the fact that it is less a learned way of prayer than one which spontaneously "flows" toward contemplation as its destination, as inevitably as the snows of mountain peaks, melted by the spring sun's warmth, descend through lakes and rivers and ultimately reach the sea. In a similar way, the progressive levels in Lectio are experienced as a unified interior movement which reaches the object of its desire fully only in the final "contemplation."

Far from being an esoteric way of prayer, intended for a sophisticated or chosen few, Lectio is in fact such a simple and effortless way of praying via sacred scripture that one wonders how, together with its attendant contemplative dimension, it ever fell into disuse and obscurity. There are many societal and historical reasons which account for the fact; they are set forth clearly and concisely by the Cistercian priest, monk and abbot, Thomas Keating, in a chapter on the history of contemplative prayer in his recent and very fine book, *Open Mind, Open Heart.*[2]

The Rediscovery of Contemplation

The fact remains that, outside the monastic orders, contemplation during the past two or three centuries was "under a cloud" and had been edged into a category considered to be only for an elite. The result was a spiritual impoverishment for the whole Church, which some have perceived as at least partially responsible for the need for renewal that resulted in the convening of the Second Vatican Council.

Today, a vital aspect of that renewal is the desire inspired in many people to grow in relationship with God. They want to learn how to respond more effectively to Jesus and to the message of his life and Gospel, which so directly address the poignant needs of our world today. In the light of those overwhelming needs, many experience a sobering sense of identification when hearing the question, "If you were on trial for being a Christian, would there be enough evidence to convict you?" For simple honesty reveals how much remains to become and to do, in order to be "convicted" Christians, true followers of Jesus. Often they have an intuitive sense that the changes called for, in themselves and in the world, will not come about through human means alone, but must be born in hearts fully opened to God and to the transforming power of his love.

In other words, without always being able to explain or define it, what many feel called to is to become "contemplatives in action." This is not an impossible ideal for today's committed Christian. Indeed, it may well be the new vocation of a great number of laypeople, whatever their state in life. For there is nothing mutually exclusive between the two terms, "contemplation" and "action"; they are in fact complementary.

Thomas Merton used an effective image to illustrate this when he wrote of "the spring and the stream." Unless the waters of the spring are living and flow outward, he said, the spring becomes only a stagnant pool. And if the stream loses contact with the spring which is its source, it dries up. In this image of Merton's, *contemplation* is the spring of living water, and *action* is the stream that flows out from it to others; it is the same water. But if action is out of touch with an interior source in prayer it eventually becomes arid and barren, and prayer that does not flow into action is cut off from life. This is the integrity of contemplation and action.

Jesus provides us with a parallel of this principle in John 7:37–39:

> On the last day, the great day of the festival, Jesus stood and cried out:
> "Let anyone who is thirsty come to me!
> Let anyone who believes in me come and drink!
> As scripture says, 'From his heart shall flow streams of living water.' "
> He was speaking of the Spirit which those who believed in him were to receive.

Add to this his words from Luke 11:13:

> If you then . . . know how to give your children what is good, how much more will the heavenly Father give the Holy Spirit to those who ask him!

The gift of the Spirit is the "living water" of contemplation and action, in the Christian whose deepest desire is to be open to the gift, and to allow God's love to be the center and guiding principle of his or her life.

Even the first stirrings of real desire for this, when not resisted but given joyful welcome and obedience, seem to gain momentum in an ongoing redirection of one's life.

Jesus' encounter with the Samaritan woman at the well is a beautiful paradigm. A simple, ordinary—even infamous—woman, while engaged in one of the prosaic tasks of her daily life, in this "chance" meeting hears him say:

> If you only knew what God is offering, you would have been the one to ask (for water), and he would have given you living water (Jn 4:10).

And though her conversation with him began with incredulity and scoffing, it concludes with the amazing revelation of his identity as the "Messiah—that is, Christ," when he says,

> That is who I am, I who speak to you (Jn 4:25–26).

Having received from Jesus "living waters,"

> the woman put down her water jar and hurried back to the town to tell the people. "Come and see . . . could this be the Christ?" This brought people out of the town and they made their way toward him (Jn 4:28–30).

After begging him to stay with them,

> He stayed for two days, and many more came to believe on the strength of the words he spoke to them; and they said to the woman, "Now we believe no longer because of what you told us; we have heard him ourselves and we know that he is indeed the Savior of the world" (Jn 4:40–42).

And so in a small town, on an ordinary day, ordinary people through an experiential encounter with Jesus were brought into a movement of new life which has changed the world forever. But the "powers of darkness" are still at work, and there is more—much more—to be done. There is a whole new and wonderful world of Christian life and ministry opening up to lay people today. A deep life of prayer and "being-for-God" can be genuinely compatible with an active and effective Christian presence in this world. To quote Thomas Merton again, the "Christ who sleeps like dynamite in your paper flesh" has totally identified with all the struggles and pains, frustrations and doubts, disappointments and failures of our life experience, and as well with our human yearning for God and faithful love. He is as intent today on teaching and leading us through his Spirit to follow him in love and total trust, as ever he was in the human life he lived at a specific time in history. And he continues to "stand at the door, knocking" until "one of you hears me calling and opens the door" (Rv 3:20).

Contemplation in Jesus

In his humanity, Jesus experienced the contemplation of his Father, and invites us, through the gift of his Spirit, to enter into that experience. It is available to us in the measure of our faith and love, which are the proximate means, in this life, of "seeing" God, of touching and being touched by him—i.e., of "experiencing" him.

In Jesus' life this prayer and action follow one another in a rhythm which seems as constant as the inhaling and exhaling of breathing. In all the Gospels there are numerous references to his custom of going "into the hills to pray," of "spending the night in prayer," of "rising before dawn to go out to a lonely place to pray." We cannot separate this prayer from his works, nor fail to see it is the very source of his teachings, his Gospel and his mission. Its contemplative nature is clearly manifest in such passages as these from John's Gospel:

> Jesus replied: "In all truth I tell you, by himself the Son can do nothing; he can do only what he sees the Father doing: and whatever the Father does the Son does too. For the Father loves the Son and shows him everything he himself does, and he will show him even greater things . . . " (5:19–20).

> Jesus answered them: "My teaching is not from myself: it comes from the one who sent me; anyone who is prepared to do his will will know whether my teaching is from God or whether I speak on my own account" (7:16–17).

> "And what I declare to the world I have learned from him." They did not recognize that he was talking to them about the

Father. So Jesus said: "What I say is what the Father has taught me" (8:26–28).

(Jesus raised his eyes to heaven and said:) "For I have given them the teaching you gave to me" (17:8).

To be a follower of Jesus, to be incorporated into him and to receive his Spirit, includes the potential of sharing in the contemplative experience. Indeed, in this sense it is our birthright as children of the same Father, and will become literally a "lifeline" of communication for his faith-filled follower.

The Ultimate Goal

This graced "seeing" of the God of Jesus, however, does not allow us to forget that we also experience him, and are to love and serve him, in our neighbor, i.e., the whole human family, as well as to recognize and respond to his presence in the immediate realities of our daily life and in the events of history and society. For contemplation is not an ultimate goal. It is still only an experiential contact with God, and we are not created for this experience, nor for any thing, however sublime; we are created for God himself. But contemplative prayer can open to us such a glimpse, such a "seeing" of God, that we might paraphrase the Old Testament text, "No one can see God and live," by adding, "as one lived before that vision." For it has the power to awaken in us such a detonation of love that we will forever feel like exiles, longing to be "at home" with him. As St. Paul writes, in part, in a beautiful passage from his second letter to the Corinthians:

It is God who designed us for this very purpose, and he has given us the Spirit as a pledge. We are always full of confidence, then, realizing that as long as we are at home in the body we are exiled from the Lord, guided by faith and not yet by sight . . . and long to be at home with (him) (2 Cor 5:1–9).

All this is grace—but it is not "cheap grace," to use Bonhoffer's phrase. The disposition which opens and readies us for the gift of contemplative prayer is already a response to a given desire to "see"

God and to be one with him in love. But it is a desire which sets us on a painful path of emptying ourselves of the self-orientation which is the major obstacle to its fulfillment. The task before us is much more a matter of subtraction than of addition (as Meister Eckhart said), for we are soon brought to realize that we are pre-occupied with ourselves.

A simple ancient fable reveals this artfully, in telling of one seeking the Beloved. He knocks at his door and hears: "Who is there?" He replies, "It is I." The response comes: "There is no room in here for both of us." Despondent, he goes away into the forest and for long months meditates on the words he has heard. Then he returns and knocks again at the door. In response to the same question, "Who is there?" he replies, "It is Thee!"—and the door opens to receive him.

The transformation of the "I" into the "Thee" in this fable indicates the prospect of a real kind of death. We begin to realize the seriousness of this imperative when we are able to suspend our defenses and really hear what Jesus is saying, in teaching that to follow him we must "deny" and "renounce" ourselves, and even "hate" and "lose" our lives, for his sake. And we begin to sense a strange inner contradiction, in discovering that what we now most long for, we most resist, and even fear. Instinctively, we try to look past those words of Jesus and go on to more consoling ones.

But the centrality of this teaching is undeniable. Usually subtitled "the doctrine of the cross" or "the condition of following Christ," it appears no less than six times in the synoptic Gospels, with very slight variations.[3] Basically, it reads as follows:

> Then, speaking to all, he said, "If anyone wants to be a follower of mine, let him renounce himself and take up his cross every day and follow me. Anyone who wants to save his life will lose it; but anyone who loses his life for my sake, will save it" (Lk 9:23–24).

It is a paradox. For isn't this the same Jesus who tells us he has come that we might have life "to the full"? And that our "joy may be full"?[4] Yet here he tells "all" and "anyone" to renounce and lose his life.

What is he really saying?

16

Because the answer to this question is crucial and at the heart of Christian spirituality and prayer, it warrants some exploration at this point.

NOTES

1. The use of the words *meditation* and *contemplation* has been further confused in recent decades with the assimilation of some Eastern methods of meditation into Christian practice. These methods, with their well-developed psychological intuitions and spiritual disciplines, have enriched our own tradition in many ways. But while they have a certain similarity to contemplation, they are basically distinct from it, and are generally referred to by both East and West as "meditation" and never as contemplation. On our side, the similarities have led to the frequent use of the word "meditation" as a synonym for contemplation. In the vocabulary of Lectio however, the two words remain distinct.

2. Thomas Keating, *Open Mind, Open Heart: The Contemplative Dimension of the Gospel* (Amity, N.Y.: Amity House, 1986), Ch. 3. Fr. Keating is a prime mover of the Centering Prayer teaching, which has a direct relationship to Lectio as we shall see later on.

3. Mt 10:38–39; 16:24–25; Mk 8:34–35; Lk 9:23–24; 14:26–27; 17:33.

4. Jn 10:10; 15:11; 16:24.

CHAPTER TWO

Dying To Live: Resolving the Paradox

In many talks on spirituality which I have given over the years to a variety of audiences, I have learned that the most predictable response of all is the immediate identification and agreement demonstrated by spontaneous head-nodding whenever I have quoted from Romans 7:

> I do not understand my own behavior; I do not act as I mean to, but I do things that I hate . . . for though the will to do what is good is in me, the power to do it is not: the good thing I want to do, I never do; the evil thing which I do not want—that is what I do" (Rom 7:15, 18b–19).

The universality of that invariable response of identification with the human dilemma so well described by St. Paul points unmistakably to our common beginnings—to our "fallen" human nature, or sin as literally "original": at the origins of our history in this world.

The Genesis myth delineates this with beautiful simplicity in the serpent's classic line of seduction: "You will be like gods" (Gen 3:5). However mysteriously humanity's assent to that temptation has been made, its consequences in our heritage are obvious and radical. This illusion of a relative omnipotence, even when not a conscious individual choice, finds us alienated: from God, from one another, from our own inner selves—and even from creation, as evidenced in the growing devastation of our environment, violated in so many ways by the effects of that same assumed omnipotence.

The True Self and the False Self

Within each one of us, an effect of that state of alienation is a confusion of identity, recognized in both theology and psychology. Thomas Merton frequently gravitates to this as a central concept of his spirituality, and the related theme of the true and false self underlies much of his writing. As early as 1956, in *The Silent Life*, he wrote:

. . . although God our Father made us free, he did not make us omnipotent. We are capable of becoming perfectly godlike, in all truth, by freely receiving from God the gift of his light, and his love, and his freedom in Christ, the incarnate Logos. But in so far as we are implicitly convinced that we ought to be omnipotent of ourselves we usurp to ourselves a godlikeness that is not ours. . . . In our desire to be "as gods"—a lasting deformity impressed in our nature by original sin—we seek what one might call a relative omnipotence: the power to have everything we want, to enjoy everything we desire, to demand that all our wishes be satisfied and that our will should never be frustrated or opposed. It is the need to have everyone else bow to our judgment and accept our declarations as law. It is the insatiable thirst for recognition of the excellence we so desperately need to find in ourselves to avoid despair. This claim to omnipotence, our deepest secret and our inmost shame, is in fact the source of all our sorrows, all our unhappiness, all our dissatisfactions, all our mistakes and deceptions. It is a radical falsity. . . . [1]

And further:

There are many acceptable and "sane" ways of indulging one's illusory claim to divine power. One can be, for example, a proud and tyrannical parent—or a tearful and demanding martyr-parent. One can be a sadistic and overbearing boss, or a nagging perfectionist. One can be a clown, or a dare-devil, or a libertine. One can be rigidly conventional, or blatantly unconventional; one can be a hermit or a demagogue. Some satisfy their desire for divinity by knowing everybody else's business: others by judging their neighbor, or telling him what to do. One can even, alas, seek sanctity and religious perfection as an unconscious satisfaction of this deep, and hidden impurity of soul which is man's pride. [2]

It is true that these negative behavioral factors may not always be overtly manifested, but they lurk in the shadows of all of us. For almost from birth, the ego, or false self, does not perceive itself as relative, but absolute. Jungian psychologist Edward Edinger states that infants "have an implicit assumption of deity."[3] And it is true that from our emergence from our mother's womb into this world, our almost immediate experiences of conscious reality proceed to confirm the illusion that we are the center of the universe: the crying infant is comforted; hungry, it is fed. Its every need is catered to for its very survival and growth; everything is given, nothing demanded of it.

This idyllic state is relatively short-lived. Though the human has one of the longest dependency spans of any species, nevertheless the illusion is challenged soon enough, when other "centers of the universe" collide with its expectations and demands. And so the long process of fabricating a defense system begins, protecting and preserving the illusion. Devious and elaborate ways are found to "get my way," often by running roughshod over others.

With this initial conditioning, the basic orientation to the satisfaction of one's selfish needs and desires is further entrenched, along with the aggression, defensiveness and claiming of rights which are created by the challenge and threat of those "others" who enter our limited world and place demands upon us. "Watch out for No. 1!" becomes an implicit and instinctive motto. This is the more overt expression of autonomy. At the opposite pole, the meek, self-effacing "people pleaser" may be acting out of the same dynamic of self-interest, though the mode of manifesting it is more subtle.

This basic egocentrism is opposed to God- and other-centeredness, and is in effect a resistance to love, the source and meaning of our being. This is why conversion may be described as a "shifting of one's center," away from narcissistic self-love and self-serving, to the self-giving love and serving of God and others—i.e., to begin to be who we really are: our true self, the image of God, who is Love.

The Human Calamity

The human calamity is that, instead, we identify with the illusory self, and not with the yet undiscovered or unaccepted goodness and beauty of the true self. Small wonder, then, that we hear and experience so much about "poor self image" and that books with titles such as *If You Really Knew Me, Would You Still Like Me?*[4] are successful—they touch a painful area of recognition.

The distortion and illusion of the superficial self, which does not accept its limits but rather claims for itself a total autonomy, lies in the assumption that it is our real identity. It is not yet differentiated from the true self, our deepest center and the ground where we meet God. It is to that center that he draws us in prayer, where we can lay claim only to what is given, not achieved. ("Who made you so important? What have you got that was not given to you? And if it was given to you, why are you boasting as though it were your own?" (1 Cor 4:7).

It is this illusion which produces the dis-ease, the unhappiness and frustration, described in the quotation from St. Paul at the beginning of this chapter. Paul continues:

> In my inmost self I dearly love God's law, but I see that acting on my body there is a different law which battles against the law in my mind. So I am brought to be a prisoner of that law of sin which lives inside my body. What a wretched man I am! Who will rescue me from this body doomed to death? (Rom 7:21–24).

The false self is the prison, from which one must escape in order to reach the true self, and God. For "If I find him, I will find myself, and if I find myself, I will find him."[5]

Paul finally answers his own question "Who will rescue me?" with:

> God—thanks be to him—through Jesus Christ our Lord (Rom 7:25).

In principle this appears to be crystal-clear—but the struggle Paul describes continues because of a mighty resistance which arises in us, not least out of the fear we sense at the prospect of a surrender which will turn our lives around and move us out of that central position of control. Instead, it appears then that:

> God is not nice
> God is not an uncle
> God is an earthquake.[6]

We want to continue to look to ourselves for security, and so we cannot give our radical trust, and completely hand ourselves over, to another—even God! As another Hasidic quotation tells us:

> How easy it is for a poor man to depend on God! What else has he to depend on? And how hard it is for a rich man to depend on God. All his possessions call out to him: "Depend on us!"[7]

It hardly needs mention that our "riches" and "possessions" may be psychological and spiritual, as well as material.

Explicit though our claims of trust in God may be, isn't it true that implicitly—even habitually—we try to make our decisions and live our lives on the basis of autonomy? To be "out of control" is perhaps the most threatening (or at least disconcerting) of prospects, for many of us. The defensive and self-protective need to be in control not only obtains in major matters, but pervades our experience as an all-inclusive attitude brought to bear on even the most ordinary affairs of day-to-day living. A wonderfully "commonplace" example of this, with which no doubt all of us can readily identify, is the following ingenuous self-observation of Elaine Prevallet:

> When I imagine my own life simple and uncomplicated, I picture my room and desk tidy, everything in its place. I myself am moving gracefully and graciously from one task to the next with precision, on schedule but with no strain or pressure. The schedule and the tasks are perfectly synchronized. It could all be so simple, I say to myself, if everything were only in its place.
>
> But it isn't. It's complicated. It's complicated because people don't stay in place. They aren't predictable, they foul up my schedule, they interfere with my agenda, they make demands I hadn't programmed. It's complicated because there is too much to do, too many tasks, too many needs, too much going

on. I can't keep up with it all; I'm always at least a step or two behind. I can't do everything that needs to be done; I feel burdened, sometimes even guilty, for being so limited. And I think maybe I'm doing it wrong, and if I could just figure out how to do it right I'd be able to meet everyone's needs. It's complicated because there's never enough time. In my anxiety to conquer time by controlling its dispensation, I feel myself victimized by it. I am unable to find time, take time, get time: all control words.

Mostly what I find is frustration. My life is out of control. I feel a need to be in control of my life and all the factors, situations, and people that complicate it. I set myself over-against them and need to dominate them, to subject them to my agenda, fit them into my program. I do have an agenda, and I don't want it interrupted. I set up my day and I offer it to God.

But there's something wrong in the picture. When I imagine—or when I experience—the simple way, everything moves in a rhythm. There is AN AGENDA, and I'm in tune with it, but it's not my creation. I don't need to worry about controlling; I don't need to be anxious that it won't all work out. I'm not in command and don't need to be. . . . The interruptions are as integral to the scene as anything I had planned. I only receive the day and the program that comes to me during the day from God. And that's what makes the difference.[8]

Self-Surrender

And so the dialectic goes on. For the prospect of transformation to a life of love has for us the intimation and attraction of an ultimate truth: it is in the surrender of my false self with its claim of full autonomy, and in letting love become the dynamic central reality of my life, that my true self will be most fully realized. But this means beginning to follow Jesus along a path which must take me in a direction directly opposite to my instinctive self-oriented choices. It is "shifting my center," away from my self, to self-giving, in love. This is precisely Jesus' meaning—that I only discover who I am and possess my true identity by "losing myself" for his sake.

For most English speaking people, the words "self-surrender" have an almost totally negative connotation. They imply a giving up, a kind of defeat, in submission or capitulation. A quite different sense is found in the French equivalent. The foundress of my congregation, St. Therese Couderc,[9] has left a spiritual legacy in the form of a monograph on self-surrender, entitled in the original French, "Se Livrer," which has the more positive meaning: to "hand or deliver oneself over to"—i.e., a freely chosen act of love. This is the axis of conversion: the total turning to God in self-donation.

What prompts this surrender and makes it possible is the realistic recognition that my very life and being is a gift of love. It is a recognition which becomes experiential in contemplative prayer, in a "knowing" that is beyond knowledge; it is the graced knowledge of love. Only such a gift can make unconditional self-surrender possible, for it is an experience of the unconditional love of a person, a personal God. It is such a recognition that breaks forth joyously in Daniel Berrigan's "All, all is gift. Give it away. Give it away."

What we are speaking about, in essence, is "falling in love."[10] It is the inescapable message of Jesus' life and teaching that the only real self-fulfillment of life is in giving it away, in love. And it is through the intimate knowledge of his life and love, learned experientially in prayer, that we begin to fathom that "Love is his meaning," in the words of the fourteenth century mystic, Julian of Norwich.[11]

Understanding such a statement intellectually is in itself powerless to change us. It is above all in the experiential faith of contemplation that we begin to embrace this truth, and that it embraces us. Then we can begin to live it in the following of Jesus, and discover, as he did, the loving God in the deep center of our own heart.

The Paradox Resolved

Let's return now to the paradox of Jesus' "doctrine of the cross" and see how the foregoing insights may reveal in it another dimension of the paschal mystery of death and resurrection.

A typical version of the six similar texts cited earlier, is the following:

> Then Jesus said to his disciples, "If anyone wants to be a follower of mine, let him renounce himself and take up his cross and follow me. Anyone who wants to save his life will lose it; but anyone who loses his life for my sake will find it" (Mt 16:24–25).

We find a strikingly different version of this teaching in the New American Bible translation of Matthew 10:38–39:

> He who will not take up his cross and come after me is not worthy of me. He who seeks only himself brings himself to ruin, whereas he who brings himself to naught for me, discovers who he is.

In the light of our development, we may now paraphrase v. 38:

> He who seeks only his illusory false self brings his true self to ruin; whereas he who brings his false self to naught for me discovers who he is—i.e., the image of God, his true self.

Thomas Merton personalizes this teaching of Jesus:

> In order to become myself I must cease to be what I always thought I wanted to be, and in order to find myself I must go out of myself, and in order to live I have to die.[12]

No wonder he once said, "Be careful if you're thinking of making friends with the Holy Spirit—because he's going to ask you to die!" He was referring to the illusion of the false self, obstacle to God, and the source of all our sorrow. The true self, gradually revealed to us in prayer, is the self created "to become love in human form."[13]

"To become love"—this is the sum and substance of Jesus' teaching, and our ultimate fulfillment: "What no eye has seen and no ear has heard, what the mind of man cannot visualize; all that God has prepared for those who love him" (1 Cor 2:9).

NOTES

1. Thomas Merton, *The Silent Life* (New York: Farrar, Straus & Giroux, fourth printing 1978), pp. 14–15.

2. *Ibid.*, p. 16.

3. E. Edinger, *Ego and Archetype* (Penguin Pelican, 1973), p. 7.

4. Eugene Kennedy, *If You Really Knew Me, Would You Still Like Me?* (Argus Communications, 1975).

5. Thomas Merton, *New Seeds of Contemplation* (New York: New Directions Publishing House, 1972), p. 36.

6. Unidentified Hasidic saying.

7. Martin Buber, *Tales of the Hasidim, Later Masters* (New York, 1947), p. 92.

8. Elaine M. Prevallet, *Reflections on Simplicity* (Pendle Hill, Pa.: Pendle Hill Publications, 1982), pp. 3–4.

9. 1805–1885; founded in France the Congregation of Our Lady of the Retreat in the Cenacle in 1826, an international religious community whose charism and ministry is "to awaken and deepen faith."

10. In *Method in Theology* (London: Darton, Longman & Todd, 1972) Bernard Lonergan has described religious conversion as "otherworldly falling in love" and "total and permanent self-surrender."

11. *The Revelations of Divine Love of Julian of Norwich*, trans. by James Walsh, S. J. (St Meinrad, Ind.: Abbey Press, 1975), Ch. 86, p. 209.

12. *New Seeds of Contemplation, op. cit.*, p. 47.

13. Brian Swimme, *The Universe Is a Green Dragon: A Cosmic Creation Story*, (Santa Fe, NM: Bear & Co., Inc., 1973), p. 40.

CHAPTER THREE

The Deepening of an Interpersonal Relationship

As far as I know, no one has ever proposed a method of falling in love. On the other hand, it doesn't just happen; there are certain preliminary conditions, even though we may initially be unaware that they are developing. For romantic novels, TV soap operas and advertising media to the contrary, love is not the product of some instantaneous magic. There are things to be cleared away, there are foundations to be laid, there is growing to be done. And its beginnings are as familiar as the principle, "We cannot love what we do not know."

Still, knowing another person is only a beginning. It might even be the end if it leads to the disillusionment of our earlier hopes. Assuming, however, that our hopes withstand the first revelations in the process of getting to know another, we have still a long way to travel together before we arrive at that mysterious and wonderful union of hearts and minds and spirits which can be called love in the deepest sense of the word.

Being "in Love"

People are capable of tremendous self-sacrifice and self-giving when they are in love. The remarkable thing is that they don't even think of it as costly—they find it the most "natural" thing in the world, and *not* to give would be a painful alternative. I suggest that the reason may be something like the dynamic of conversion commented on earlier—there has been a "shifting of one's center." The center of the person's life has become the beloved.

I remember well the strange behavior of my "big brother," eight years my senior, when his wife-to-be came into his life. They were seniors together in high school. He seemed always preoccupied; he spent less and less time at home. He began to dress differently; he looked different! He came home late from school, and even later from his "dates." At our Sunday family dinner, the one occasion of the week when all four of us were together at a meal (because of my father's business), Ralph would push back his chair—*before* dessert!—saying, "May I be excused?" After a while my father stopped asking "Where are you going?" He knew.

I suppose everyone knows the usual progression of events: we met the girl, our respective families met, holidays were spent together, and happily everyone approved of everyone else. There were few things in Ralph's life which were not affected by the new love affair. Before plans for marriage could be made, time and money had to be provided for further education, and sacrifices were made for that. Ralph went to work and paid his own way to an engineering degree, supported loyally meanwhile by his fiancée, who also worked and saved. It was a long engagement, and that was also a sacrifice! Meanwhile there were many changes in my brother himself; even his "kid sister" thought he was nicer somehow. He was certainly happier and easier to live with. No doubt there was nothing really unusual about the sequence of events: the long awaited marriage, the saving and sacrificing to have a "home of their own," all the joys and trials and rewards of having children, and providing all over again for *their* future. Joys and sorrows, births and deaths, successes and failures, misunderstandings and reconciliations—and through it all a constant growth in oneness and maturing love, in a life shared from beginning to end, because they were "in love."

Lectio Divina: A Continuum

There are many parallels and conclusions which can be drawn between the evolution of such a love relationship and the evolution of the love relationship with God which develops in prayer. First and most evident: it takes time! In both relationships, we're inclined to look to the accomplishment of goals—in the first instance, getting married, buying a home, having children—all "ends," which we finally realize are the means that constitute the ongoing journey together, the sharing of life, in love and faithfulness. So too in prayer, the "end" is not some imagined degree of contemplation, or a mystical experience that will tell us we've arrived, but "joys and sorrows, births and deaths, successes and failures, misunderstandings and reconciliations—and through it all a constant growth in oneness and maturing love, in a life shared from beginning to end."

Lectio is like that. It is not a "method" of prayer, but rather parallels that human experience of the development of a deeply loving interpersonal relationship, and follows the same dynamic, illustrating how "grace builds on nature." For we grow in love of God as we grow in any intimate love relationship—through a continuum of knowing, trusting, desiring, surrendering our defenses and fears, and ultimately our very selves, to the Beloved. That continuum corresponds with the deepening levels of prayer which are encompassed in the process of Lectio with its four progressive phases, flowing from reflection on the word of scripture to spontaneous prayer and then to a silent presence to God in love.

St. John of the Cross's paraphrase of a verse from St. Luke's Gospel (11:9) provides us with an outline of the four steps of Lectio:

Seek in READING,
and you will find in MEDITATION;
knock in PRAYER
and it will be opened to you
in CONTEMPLATION.

In exploring these four phases or movements—reading (*lectio*), meditation (*meditatio*), prayer (*oratio*), and contemplation (*contemplatio*)—we will soon appreciate how the element of "wholeness" characterizes Lectio, for it engages the whole person: mind, heart and spirit—the intellect and imagination, the will and the affections. All are at some point activated by grace, reaffirming the fact that Lectio Divina is not an objective technique to be learned and followed as a system which will "produce" deep prayer. On the contrary, it is an organic process, which takes place over a period of time, both in the *microcosm* of a single prayer period, and in the *macrocosm* of a lifetime engagement with God in the lived prayer of faithful love.

While leading to contemplative prayer as its fruition, Lectio incorporates within a unified unfolding movement those forms of prayer which only as late as the sixteenth century were separated into distinct categories—namely, discursive prayer (or meditation), affective prayer (or "prayer of the heart"), and contemplation (or "mystical" prayer). In Lectio, these are spontaneous and integrated, in an orientation toward progressively greater simplicity and depth, the realm of contemplation. We have evidence here again that the tradition of centuries assumed contemplation was not an exclusive privilege of an elect few, but was the normal fulfillment of prayer, available to all genuine Christians willing to dedicate themselves to a serious following of Jesus.

The form that discipleship takes is conditioned by the historic times in which one lives, as well as by the context of an individual's life, but the underlying principle remains: each of us is called by love to love; called out of our narrow individualism and our small private world, to allow ourselves to be "turned around" by the allurement of God, and to *live for him,* as Jesus did. To follow Jesus is to be in love, with all that is consequent upon that gift. When that love is fully accepted our lives begin to change from the center.

The Grace of Accepted Love

It makes little difference what treasure we may have clung to, what seduction we may have succumbed to, what resistance we may have energized in ourselves, to block our total surrender to God. There remains within us a love that can be awakened by the sheer grace of his love's desire for us, *if we fully accept it.* Yet, as we all know, we find this incredibly difficult. Perhaps this is why the observation has been made that most of us seem to assume that union with God is attained by laboriously ascending a ladder of virtues, which finally fashion our holiness and make us fit for him. In truth, the reverse is far more accurate: the great saints and mystics have been those who fully accepted *God's* love for *them.* It is this which makes everything else possible. Our incredulity in the face of God's immense love, and also self-hate or an unyielding sense of guilt, can be formidable obstacles to God's love, and are often subtle and unrecognized forms of pride, in putting our "bad" above his mercy.

In the field of psychiatry this has also been clearly recognized, as noted by Dominic Rover, O.P.: "Psychiatry yields up the prime insight that loving acceptance as we are known, as we are revealed, in our misery and disorder, is what we all crave, even as we are inclined, tragically, to disbelieve it."

The late Protestant theologian, Paul Tillich, went so far as to say that the meaning of faith is "To accept the fact that I am accepted, in my total unacceptability."

Finally, a fascinating light on this total acceptance of love can be found in the reflections of some theologians today on the possibility that Jesus himself experienced a profound conversion at the time of his baptism by John—a conversion not from sin to virtue (which is unthinkable in him) but in the radical redirection of his life, in which his entire person was caught up in such a total and unconditional response to the revelation he received of the Father's love for him "at once, as he was coming up out of the water," that his entire human existence was irrevocably turned toward the Father, with all the intensity of his being.

This view would seem to be supported by what we know of his life through scripture. Such a conversion would explain, for example, the astonishment of his fellow townsmen who knew him in the years before his baptism:

> When Jesus had finished these parables he left the district; and, coming to his home town, he taught the people in their synagogue in such a way that they were astonished and said, "Where did the man get this wisdom and these miraculous powers? This is the carpenter's son, surely? Is not his mother the woman called Mary, and his brothers James and Joseph and Simon and Jude? His sisters, too, are they not all here with us? So where did the man get it all?" And they would not accept him (Mt 13:53–57a).

We can only conclude from this that a striking change had unaccountably taken place in Jesus, in "wisdom and power." This conclusion is strongly suggested by Jesus as well in his answer to the challenge of the chief priests and elders:

He had gone into the temple and was teaching, when the chief priests and the elders of the people came to him and said, "What authority have you for acting like this? And who gave you this authority?" In reply Jesus said to them, "And I will ask you a question, just one; if you tell me the answer to it, then I will tell you my authority for acting like this. *John's baptism,* what was its origin, heavenly or human?" (Mt 21:23–25a).

This would also place in a new perspective the nature of the temptations in the desert which followed Jesus' baptism, for then it appears that even Jesus had to struggle to integrate the unconditional acceptance of this overwhelming experiential revelation of the Father's love, described in Mark 1:9–11:

> It was at this time that Jesus came from Nazareth in Galilee and was baptized in the Jordan by John. And at once, as he was coming up out of the water, he saw the heavens torn apart and the Spirit, like a dove, descending on him. And a voice came from heaven, "You are my Son, the Beloved; my favor rests on you."

We can hardly imagine the interior reverberations of such a revelation in the heart of Jesus, indicated in the symbolic language of this text, as "he saw the heavens torn apart." Indeed in the next verse (v. 12) it follows, "And at once the Spirit *drove* him into the desert."

The point of particular relevance for us, made in all the foregoing, is the absolute and primary importance of an unconditional acceptance of God's love, if we are to become all he has created and called us to be. John writes in his first epistle, "Let us love, then, because *he first* loved us" (1 Jn 4:19). To fail to accept this is to deny our true identity, indeed the very reason for our being, and to resist the tide of God's creative love which would carry us to completion in him.

The full knowledge of this love, which is God's presence in us, can never be grasped by our intellect; it is literally incomprehensible. But as the author of *The Cloud of Unknowing* writes,

> He whom neither men nor angels can grasp by knowledge *can be embraced by love.* For the intellect of both men and angels is too small to comprehend God as he is in himself.[1] (Italics added)

This is the "loving knowledge" which in part defines contemplative prayer, and which becomes experiential in contemplation. Lectio Divina prepares the way to it, with an attentive listening of the heart, leading to an inner awakening to God's *hesed*, his faithful love, present within us and the answer to our nameless longing.

Some Prerequisites for Lectio Divina

Before beginning to comment on the first of Lectio Divina's four steps or movements, some important points should be made. First, the experience of this movement is not a programmed or automatic 1-2-3-4 progression. From the first step we are entering into a "flow" which has an inner direction, and its course will be unique to each time of prayer. Over a period of time we may find, for example, that there will be occasions as we prepare for prayer when we are almost immediately drawn into a deep sense of God's loving presence, before we have even opened a page or reflected on it. At other times we may enter into a profound silence, without prelude. These are movements of grace, and we will never be "in charge" in prayer if it is real.

We can't presume such graciousness, however, and idle away the time in vacuous expectancy, much less attempt to manipulate it by some technique or formula. Prayer is always gift. Lectio is an attempt not to fabricate it, but to enable us to respond to the gift from its first invitation, and to dispose ourselves for its development. We can bring no "timetable" of our own to the process. We will discover this in those times when all we can do is wait, while the Holy Spirit teaches us by the experience of our helplessness things more important than consolation or ecstasy. For the more prayer is *received*, rather than *made*, the more genuine it will be.

If we have done our best in all simplicity to be present and open to the Spirit in the desire of faith and love, we must trust that God will draw good from all in his own way and time. We really cannot evaluate our prayer, except by its long-term effects in our daily living. The one thing of which we can be absolutely certain is that he knows our heart and is faithful. Meanwhile, we go to prayer to give ourselves in love, and not as mercenaries seeking rewards.

Second, prayer can never be dissociated from our everyday life, which is the arena for the ongoing conversion discussed in Chapter Two. It will be by means of our daily experiences and relationships that God will continue to "flesh out"—i.e., incarnate—through people and events his grace of gradual transformation. We cannot accomplish this through our own efforts. Rather, our part is one of consent, and of letting go of all that resists him, arising from the illusions of the false self in its egocentricity and claims to autonomy. Our conversion to love as the dynamic central reality of our life, living to give rather than to get—which is the way of Jesus—is not the end result of our own resolution and effort. That would be simply another assertion of the false self in pious disguise. Anyone who has made retreat or New Year's resolutions recognizes how ineffective and even counterproductive this can be. It is our "yes" to God, usually at the cost of another "death" to the false self, which opens the way to new life in the Spirit. "Ongoing conversion" is the experience of the paschal mystery, and Jesus has shown us the way, described by Paul:

> The Son of God, Jesus Christ . . . was never Yes-and-No; his nature is all Yes. For in him is found the Yes to all God's promises and therefore it is "through him" that we answer "Amen" to give praise to God (2 Cor 1:19–21).

In the "now" of each day and moment we will never lack opportunity to live the "Yes, Amen" which was the love-induced response of our prayer; in this way prayer and action find their integrity. Without such recognition and response we run the risk of illusion. Of course we will often fail, in the struggle to be faithful to the desire to say our "Yes." But the sincerity of our desire is more meaningful in God's view than its accomplishment, and our experience of weakness can often teach us much more about our radical dependency upon God than our apparent and often secretly self-gratifying "successes." Thomas Keating has some wise advice on this point:

> Don't be discouraged or indulge in guilt feelings. Failure is the path to boundless confidence in God. Always remember that you have a billion chances. This God of ours is not crossing off

anything on our list of opportunities. He keeps approaching us from every possible angle. He lures, draws, nudges, or pushes us, as the case may demand, into the place where he wants us to be.[2]

Third, since the vehicle of the way of Lectio Divina is traditionally scripture (although its principles may be applied to other compatible spiritual readings), it follows that the more we are imbued with this word of God and the greater our familiarity with it, the more fruitful this way of prayer can be for us. On the other hand there are no doubt many of us who have been exposed to scripture for years who might wish at times that we could read it again as though for the first time. I believe it was G. K. Chesterton who said that if we could read the Gospels this way, we "would feel as though a millstone had rolled over us," so powerful would their impact be. Generally speaking, however, it is important for anyone desirous of growing in relationship with God to make a practice of reading scripture daily, if at all possible. As Jesus reminds us in Matthew's Gospel (4:4):

"Scripture says: 'Human beings live not on bread alone but on every word that comes from the mouth of God.' "

And finally, in beginning to pray (even before the first step of *Lectio*) we must endeavor to come to it with some realization of what it means to "dare" to pray. How wonder-full it is that I, as creature, may in truth turn to God, already present within me, with confidence that the offering of myself is anticipated by his love and mercy. As Abraham Heschel said, "There is something far greater than my desire to pray—that is, God's desire that I pray."

The deepest level of my relationship with him is where I recognize the truth of my nothingness and helplessness before him, where I am totally dependent upon him for my very existence. In the words of Thomas Merton, "Our vocation is to glorify God by our contingency"—i.e., by the acknowledgement that I cannot continue to be, except in him and because of his constantly creating love. This should be a truly joyful recognition for me, for it is the source of all life and hope.

Perhaps the best summation of our true stance before him in

prayer may be found in two basic notions of Karl Rahner's theology:

—the human person as
   the mystery of infinite emptiness, and
—God as
   the mystery of infinite fullness.

These two concepts, brought together, constitute the underlying mystery of all genuine prayer.

NOTES

1. *The Cloud of Unknowing,* trans. by William Johnston (Garden City, N.Y.: Image Books, Doubleday & Co., Inc., 1973), p. 50.

2. *Op. cit.,* pp. 74–75.

CHAPTER FOUR

Lectio Divina

1. Lectio: Reading and Listening to the Word of God

The first step of Lectio Divina is *Lectio,* or reading. It is not ordinary reading, either as to matter or manner. The matter is the "Divine Word," or scripture,[1] and the manner of reading is, more accurately, a "listening" and a "hearing," attuned to the inspired word and attentive to the Speaker.

Today we have a more expanded understanding than in former times of what is meant in speaking of scripture as "the inspired word of God." The phrase was once understood in a restricted sense: that the writers of scripture were directly inspired by the Spirit to inscribe God's word—a kind of "divine dictation." But the Spirit whom Jesus promised the Father would send in his name to dwell within us is the same Spirit who vivifies the word of scripture.[2] It is my active *faith* in this Spirit, present in the word *and* in me, which, when brought to the reading and hearing of scripture, "in-spires" or "breathes into" it[3] the living reality of the Speaker.

Therefore I prepare for this sacred reading by taking time to quiet my body and mind, in order to begin to bring my whole person into a single focus. Concerning my body: in every prayer discipline, East and West, the one consistent principle common to all is that the spine must be erect, but not tense. Whether sitting on the floor or a cushion, with legs crossed or folded, or on a straight-backed chair, the basic idea is not to impede circulation or breathing, while remaining fully attentive and alert. All such preliminaries are means to help me come to an awareness and conviction of faith that I am about to listen to the *living* word of God, intimately present to me. In this disposition, I choose a text—preferably short—and read it *slowly,* listening to it interiorly with full attention. This is already the beginning of my response to a person, who calls me to open my mind and heart to him. Sometimes the text which attracts me may be one already present, haunting my heart; perhaps it will have been suggested by a recent liturgy. Or I may make use of the "Scripture Themes" section in this book, provided specifically for this purpose in a form designed to resonate with a sense of God's present call. In all, my goal is to personalize the words, to real-ize them, as God speaking to *me, now.*

As an example, let's assume that a text (Is 65:1–2) from the Scripture Theme on "Contrition and Mercy"[4] has attracted me. After the preparations suggested, I begin the *Lectio,* or reading. I "hear" the Lord saying to me,

> I have let myself be found by those who did not seek me. I said "Here I am." . . . Each day I stretched out my hands to a rebellious people (Is 65:1–2).

It is very possible that even a text as short as this may have a different significance or import for me each time I turn to it, when I hear it in faith, for the Lord will speak to me where I am. For example, what might strike me is a realization that he *lets* himself be found, even though my seeking is flawed by selfishness, and this suddenly awakens in me a sense of unworthiness and gratitude. Or the three words, "Here I am," may resound with an unexpected immediacy and a new realization of the constancy of his presence to me.

When in "hearing" scripture we are receptive to the One who speaks in us, what we hear may be more than the words in themselves convey. The Spirit who vivifies them is himself the meaning, expressed *through* the words even more than by them, just as a lover may convey volumes in a phrase that would be mere convention when spoken by another. I have observed this time and time again in directing retreats, when the same text is heard by each individual in a wholly unique way, very often a way I never expected or imagined beforehand.

There are innumerable potentials in this text, for instance, which grace may reveal. It is also true that because this is gratuitous and not a product of my own logical deduction, it can happen that the words "leave me cold." I might then just peacefully let one phrase— such as "Here I am"—repeat itself over and over in my consciousness, and welcome it in faith. In such case, simply "being with" the

Lord in a disposition of love and trust will be sufficient, especially when realizing that of myself I can do nothing else. In fact, this realization might quite possibly be the real fruit of this time of prayer. However, if (as first suggested) I have been drawn to a particular phrase, and I am beginning to reflect on its meaning for me, then I have begun to enter into the next step, *Meditatio*.

2. Meditatio: Reflecting on the Word

Earlier, Lectio Divina was described as "the deepening of an interpersonal relationship." In this process, the role of *Lectio* just described is analogous to coming to meet the other, with the intention of sharing in time together alone. It is for this reason that I have made space in my life and turned toward God, anticipating an exchange between us which will be a deepening of our growing relationship.

Now, in the *Meditatio* to which this desire has drawn me, I want to know more about him, to welcome him into my life and open up to him, in greater trust and confidence—I want to learn who he really is for me and what he wants to reveal to me. An analogy may be helpful here, concerning this revelation.

Suppose I were in a bookstore and happened to open a book written in Greek, or Japanese, or Hebrew. I would not only not know the alphabet or the language, I wouldn't even know whether it was to be read from back to front, from bottom to top, or from left to right. It would, in other words, be "a closed book" for me, no matter how much I might want to understand it. But if a clerk happened by and, sensing my dilemma, volunteered that the same book was available in an English translation which he then handed to me, I could immediately connect with the meaning conveyed on every page.

So too, God in himself is "another language" for us, for he is incomprehensible, in his fullness, to our finite human intellect and understanding. But he has translated himself into our humanity, in Jesus. In this man, who lived and experienced to its greatest possible depths the human life we share, God stands revealed to me in flesh and blood. Jesus *is* the revelation of God, in a language I can understand and in a person I can know and love, not only as one who lived and died in history, but one who lives now, in my world, in my heart, and forever. And through the promised gift of the Spirit, which has been given, he truly speaks to me.

I suggest that before continuing your reading here, you pause to reflect prayerfully for a few moments on the following remarkable passages from the 14th chapter of John's Gospel, and try to hear them as though for the first time, *addressed to you*. To emphasize this personalization, you might insert your own name at the asterisks.

(Jesus says:)
"I am the Way; I am Truth and Life.
No one can come to the Father except through me.
If you know me, (*) you will know my Father too.
From this moment you know him and have seen him (v. 7).

I shall ask the Father,
and he will give you another Paraclete
to be with you forever,
the Spirit of truth
whom the world can never accept
since it neither sees nor knows him;
but you know him, (*)
because he is with you, he is in you (vv. 16–17).

The Paraclete, the Holy Spirit,
whom the Father will send in my name,
will teach you everything
and remind you of all I have said to you (v. 26).[5]

Before beginning this (or any) prayer, it is of primary importance to take time to be mindful of the faith dimension one is entering. When Moses approached the burning bush, "God spoke to him, saying, 'Take off your sandals, for the place where you are standing is holy ground. I am the God of your ancestors . . . ' (and) at this Moses covered his face" (Ex 3:5–6). In some comparable interior or exterior way we too must acknowledge the holiness of the God we approach, recognizing the wonder and mystery of the gift of faith which enables us to consciously come before him in prayer. It is amazing, on reflection, that we can often so casually assume that it is "of course" possible to *communicate with God!* It is important at the beginning therefore to realize—make real—the truth that prayer is always a gifted *response* to the loving initiative of the Holy Spirit. And since all prayer is his gift, it is appropriate that we ask for what we seek. In the excerpt from John's Gospel quoted above, it might be to claim the promise of Jesus by asking the Holy Spirit to teach me how to open my mind and heart to hear and understand what Jesus is saying to me.

Each person's prayer relationship with the Lord is unique. One reason for this is that there is a variety of personal gifts. In some, the imaginative faculty is more developed and active, and for such people the use of imagery may be very helpful to bring their meditation alive. In this approach, called "contemplation" in the *Spiritual Exercises* of St. Ignatius (but with a meaning different from the classical one we are using) one enters by means of imagination into a Gospel scene, seeing and hearing the persons, imagining the touch and smells of the environment, etc. I might identify with some person in the scene, or be present there as myself, watching, listening, experiencing what is going on. For example, in the excerpt from John's Gospel just quoted my imagination might be used in recreating the scene—in this instance, the gathering of Jesus with his friends at the Last Supper. And so I hear these words of Jesus addressed *to me,* and I receive his gaze *with my own eyes.* What do I see in those eyes as he speaks to me? And how shall I respond?

One whose imagination is not so active or well developed but who is perhaps more intuitive might gain more by savoring the truth or insight inherent in the passage, deeply interiorizing what Jesus is saying by allowing his words to repeat themselves slowly again and again, in the depths of the heart, until it is deeply penetrated with Jesus' assuring love, and spontaneously responds in kind.

Whatever our approach to prayer a basic principle applies which is succinctly summed up by Dom Chapman, a famous Benedictine spiritual director of the early 1900's: *"Pray as you can, not as you can't!"* For the simplest of words, when genuine and sincere—or even no words at all when the heart is too full—are surely more eloquent than the most lyrical rhetoric which is fabricated or borrowed. And most obvious of all, but perhaps for that reason easily overlooked, I must often *ask* the Spirit to teach me to pray.

I am leaving *Meditatio* at this point without further development because it would be misleading to appear to provide a detailed "how to" manual, concerning what is essentially an interior movement whose whole authenticity depends upon our being spontaneous and real. Ultimately, only the Holy Spirit can teach us to pray, and whatever anyone else may offer can only be of help in aiding us to dispose ourselves to *receive* that teaching experientially. To return to our original analogy of "being in love," it is love that teaches us to love, and it follows no objective method.

It is when this love of God touches our heart that we are drawn into the next level: *Oratio,* or prayer. All else has been a preliminary, for this is the real beginning of prayer.

3. *Oratio: The Word Touches the Heart*

Meditation, the subject of the preceding section, has an important role to play in forming us as Christians. It helps us to grow in our knowledge of God's constant work of love in all creation, and in our own individual lives; it increases and enriches our familiarity with the life and teachings of Jesus and our love for him, and leads us to reflect on how we should respond to his call in love and service. All this not only has value in itself, but also helps to establish the essential foundations of faith and conviction for our Christian life.

However, meditation is largely an activity of our intellect and imagination about God, and if it remains on an intellectual level it falls short of genuine prayer. For the goal of prayer is not thoughts or concepts or knowledge *about* God, however sublime, but God himself as he *is,* mysteriously hidden in my deepest, true self. In the language of the mystics, "God is my *me.*"[6]

This deepest center is the realm of contemplation, and *Oratio* or "prayer of the heart" which we will now consider is the beginning of the path that leads to it. Because this beginning is not predetermined by our own programming, what follows is not an "instruction"—something to *do* which will lead to the next thing to do, like an ascending stairway; it simply begins to describe what eventually becomes a spontaneous movement of the heart, when responsive to the leading of the Spirit.

Few quotations of the saints are more universally familiar than St. Augustine's "O God, our hearts are made for thee, and they shall be restless until they rest in thee!" It seems to be generally acknowledged as a truism, and resonates with an inner longing that lies not far below our surface consciousness. It is this intrinsic longing which is awakened in prayer when we allow ourselves to be vulnerable and, putting aside our defenses and masks, stand before God in our naked need and creaturehood. The time comes when we realize that this longing is itself the presence of God's longing in us. Meanwhile, *Oratio* is the active effort we make to keep our hearts open to him and to put ourselves at the disposal of his Spirit, preparing the way for God's action to supersede our own.

Over a long period of time we may find ourselves moving between meditation and this prayer of the heart, but eventually a gradual simplification begins to take place. There is less and less reasoning and speculating with the intellect, as the heart takes over in a simple pouring out of love and desire, which may take the form of an intimate interior dialogue. Sensing that God is "so near, and yet so far," the longing of our heart spontaneously calls out to him, or, realizing its infidelity and unworthiness, begs healing and mercy. All the foolish promises of a lover may be made and become one's secret with God.

In this prayer, our hearts are opened to him and by him, so that his light may enter. Because he loves us too much to leave us in our illusions, which are obstacles to his grace, sooner or later they will begin to be revealed to us for what they are: the conscious and unconscious claims of the false self to autonomy, self-sufficiency, control, pride, role playing, or limits to our generosity. The list is unique to each, but its effect is the same, to impede the life of grace and the gifts of the Holy Spirit within us. Here again the way of God seems paradoxical, for while this process of "disillusionment" now beginning is necessarily painful to us, it is a great grace of his love, for when we cooperate it will undo the dominance of the false self and center us in the true self, "the image and likeness of God" within us. If we fail to act upon whatever he is revealing or asking of us, our prayer will be to that extent untruthful. This does not mean so much that a perfect response to him is required, as that our intention and endeavor to respond are sincere. In the consoling and encouraging words of *The Cloud of Unknowing,*

> It is not what you are nor what you have been that God sees with his all-merciful eyes, but what you desire to be. (The author goes on to say:) St. Gregory declares that "all holy desires heighten in intensity with the delay of fulfillment, and desire which fades with delay was never holy desire at all."[7]

This increase of "holy desire" is one of the effects of *Oratio*. By it God creates in us a greater capacity for himself, not only by our longing but sometimes through the very frustration and powerlessness we experience as we reach out blindly toward him. It is as though we are being drawn by a magnetic force in our own depths, toward God as our center of gravity, where that center coincides with our true self. The drawing will be experienced as more powerful the more we consent to the surrender of the illusions which hinder the process of ongoing conversion: a more total turning to God as our true center, to live for him. It is a work which not only takes place in prayer, but issues from it into the concrete particulars of everyday life in our reactions and responses to others and to events.

The dynamic of such conversion is described in John the Baptist's imperative: "He must increase, I must decrease." The positive side of this Gospel principle is clarified in recalling the "true self/false self" interpretation in Chapter Two. In that context we might paraphrase: "My true self must increase, my false self must decrease." The arena, or sphere of struggle, is both interior and exterior. In the former the struggle is to surrender to God's action in prayer, and in the latter to act, to concretize that surrender in daily life—two sides of the same coin.

In *Oratio,* until we learn to be at home with the patient waiting for God that prayer will eventually teach us, we may find it helpful to return now and then to *Lectio* with a few simple words from scripture, such as the opening verse of Ps 42:

> As a deer yearns
>   for running streams,
> so I yearn
>   for you, my God.

However we must be careful not to substitute reading for prayer, for at this stage of *Oratio* we will gradually be brought to a more subtle and intuitive awareness of God which dawns slowly, and ought not to be obscured by our own impatient search for the lesser light of our limited intellectual faculties. Teresa of Avila provides a helpful example here. She tells us that when a small fire has been lighted (in our prayer), to keep it burning we may from time to time place upon it a twig or two, (e.g., a few words from scripture), but, she cautions us, we should not throw *branches* on it (lengthy reading or activity of the mind) because this will extinguish the flame.

It is difficult to give an example of this prayer of *Oratio,* because it is the unique and spontaneous voice of the heart which is touched by God and reaches out to him in ardent love. Here, we are at the third of the four levels of Lectio Divina, poetically described by Dom Marmion (a French Benedictine monk of an earlier era) as follows:

We read	(*Lectio*)
under the eye of God	(*Meditatio*)
until the heart is touched	(*Oratio*)
and leaps to flame.	(*Contemplatio*)

In terms of the analogy used earlier—the ongoing development of a deeply loving intimate human relationship—we now not only love (God) but are beginning to "fall *in* love"; i.e., he is becoming the realized center of our lives, and we begin to experience the long-ing of lovers for union: the desire to be totally given, and totally received.

Here again our daily life must parallel our prayer if it is to be au-thentic. The self-gift to which we are called in prayer must have its coextension in our daily relationships. However imperfect this may be, our desire and effort must be sincere.

The Transition to Contemplation

Thus far, in the three successive levels of *Lectio, Meditatio* and *Oratio,* while moving toward greater depth we are still in a realm where our activity has remained a dominant factor. The transition to the final *Contemplatio,* or contemplation (which is not a terminus but a new and crucial beginning), is very unlike what one might have expected. For while we are moving toward God who is Light, our *experience* seems to contradict this when a kind of darkness or "night" comes upon us, and our path becomes obscure.

What is happening is that God is taking over more and more by "closing down" our natural facilities of reason and imagination, and taking away the affective feelings of satisfaction and fervor. The result is a marked inability to think and reason about God, together with a kind of drying up of devotion and feeling. The desert has begun, and at its edge some wise guidance is crucial if we are to understand how to proceed, and not be tempted to just give it all up, not realizing we are on the threshold of a great but unrecognized promise.

The acknowledged master of this journey through the night to a new dawn is St. John of the Cross. His writings on the subject, however, are detailed and rather convoluted, reappearing in varied forms in *The Ascent of Mount Carmel, The Dark Night* and *The Living Flame of Love.* Therefore I will attempt to briefly summarize and bring together the main points which pertain here.

The Three "Signs" of John of the Cross

First, he gives three signs for discerning whether the darkness and aridities experienced are valid indications of the direct intervention of the Spirit, or if they are merely a result of some other cause, such as one's own laxity or indisposition.

1. The realization that one cannot make discursive meditation or receive satisfaction or consolation from it as before. (N.B.: As long as one can, meditation should not be abandoned.)
2. A disinclination to fix the imagination or sense faculties upon

other particulars concerning God; i.e. there is no longer any satisfaction with any *ideas* of God, for the distinction between God in himself, and concepts of him, is now realized. At this point we feel no affection for any mental image or concept of God, and all sensible consolation which was associated with his presence has evaporated. A great distress is experienced, together with a fear that we've regressed or have lost our way, and are incapable of praying at all. What we feel now, unaccountably, is only a distaste for the things of God. This is disturbing, and taken for "lukewarmness," but, as is obvious to any knowledgeable spiritual counselor, this very distress betrays a genuine concern, for were one really lukewarm such concern would not exist.

3. The third and surest sign is decisive, because the first and second might be experienced due to depression, or dissipation, or a simple lack of earnestness. But when all three signs are present together, John asserts that one may be sure that they proceed from God. This sign is that despite the inability to meditate, and the lack of satisfaction in anything else, one nevertheless has an attraction to remain alone in a simple loving awareness of God, in interior peace and quiet and repose, without any particular knowledge or understanding, or acts of the intellect, memory and will, and prefers to remain only in the general loving awareness and knowledge mentioned.

How To Proceed

St. John then gives specific advice as to how we should conduct ourselves, once this transition from our activity in prayer is indicated. He notes how easy it is to mistakenly impair God's work by our own efforts, and says that to try is to be like someone who, having reached the end of his journey, continues to walk in order to reach the end, adding, "He will necessarily move away from that end, besides doing something ridiculous."

Rather, he says, we should allow ourselves to remain in quietude, even though it may seem that we are "doing nothing" and wasting time, and even that we are somehow at fault in this. We are to be content simply with a loving and peaceful attentiveness to God, without the concern, the effort and the desire to taste or feel him, for these desires disquiet and distract us from what is secretly being communicated to us by the direct action of God. The time has come for *receiving*, for a "receptive passivity" that is far from idleness, however much it may seem so to us. A bit of Zen wisdom applies here:

Sitting still,
doing nothing,
Spring comes
and the grass grows by itself.

Though we seem to be inactive, grace is taking its course and the work of the Spirit is proceeding without our distinct knowledge.

St. John then makes it clear that those beginning to have this general loving knowledge are not *always* incapable of some return to meditation, for the transition is not immediate or total but usually takes place over a considerable period of time, until contemplation is habitual—i.e., when every time we intend to meditate we immediately notice this knowledge and peace, as well as our lack of ability or desire to meditate. Then, he cautions, if we persist in trying to consider and understand particular things, we will hinder the simple light of the Spirit and interfere, with our cloudy thoughts.

Just how long it takes cannot be predicted, for God deals uniquely with each person, but little by little, he assures us, "the divine calm and peace with a wondrous, sublime knowledge of God, enveloped in divine love, will be infused into (one's) soul," for "this contemplation is active while the soul is in idleness and unconcern. It is like air that escapes when one tries to grasp it in one's hand." "At this time a person's own efforts are of no avail, but an obstacle to the interior peace and work God is producing in the spirit through that dryness of sense."

A short resume of the main points made may be useful here:

The three signs:

1. Inability to meditate as before.
2. Lack of interest in ideas of God, usually accompanied by fear of losing one's way or regressing. Aridity of the senses.
3. (Decisive when present with 1 and 2) Attraction to solitary prayer—attentive, general and loving, but obscure; "passive attention."

What To Do

——To *receive,* and place no obstacle to the Holy Spirit.
——Follow attraction to interior silence and remain in loving attentiveness.
——Abandon all activity and let oneself be drawn into the darkness of God's love, forgetful of self.
——When it becomes possible to meditate again, do so, until and unless interior silence becomes habitual.

I have focused to this extent on the transition from "prayer of the heart" to contemplation for two important reasons. First, because without a clear understanding of what is happening, our best intentions may be misdirected and oppose, rather than follow, the attraction of the Spirit in prayer. St. John is vehement in his condemnation of those spiritual directors who "like a blacksmith know no more than to hammer and pound with the faculties" (of reason and imagination, etc.) and so contradict the unperceived movement of the Spirit. "These directors should reflect that they themselves are not the chief agent, guide and mover of souls in this matter, but that the principal guide is the Holy Spirit."

Second, this area of transition from *Oratio* to *Contemplatio* was the abortive "cutting-off place" in the spirituality of prayer that was taught beginning around the sixteenth century, as mentioned in the early part of this book. Its result was to isolate contemplation from what was considered normal prayer, and to set it apart in a category for rare "chosen souls" only.

While no such exterior institutional attitude or Church imposition prevails today, there is still another real possibility that contemplation may be resisted or excluded from the prayer of Christians, as an *effect* of the mindset of our contemporary Western society. This technological age and all its achievements of the pragmatic intellect are not without price. The mastery of much of the material world is often gained at the expense of the development of the intuitive faculties, which are directly involved in contemplation. As a result, many people are prone to inhibit and/or delay the spontaneous development of contemplation by an acquired and stubborn tendency to endlessly intellectualize, analyze, judge, and in general be "in charge" during prayer. This is in direct opposition to the inner movement of contemplation, which demands the letting go of any effort to be in control. The passive receptivity it requires, while actually creative and responsive, appears in the practical view to be a sheer waste of time. Therefore there is need for a clear understanding of what will be experienced and required of us, particularly at this point of transition from prayer of the heart to contemplation.

"Centering prayer," which is an effective modern adaptation of the teaching of *The Cloud of Unknowing,* is specifically aimed at bypassing this prevalent intellectual snag in what should be a spontaneous flowing movement: from reading and reflection, to prayer of the heart, to the interior silence of contemplation. Anyone who experiences particular difficulty with this intellectualizing in prayer will find Thomas Keating's book *Open Mind, Open Heart* (cited earlier) extremely helpful as a continuing guide. The author is founder of the centering prayer movement, and brings to it a rich contemplative tradition.

4: *Contemplatio: Entering the Silence* *"Too Deep for Words"*

Contemplation is a strange new land, where everything natural to us seems to be turned upside down—where we learn a new language (silence), a new way of being (not to *do* but simply to *be*), where our thoughts and concepts, our imagination, senses and feelings are abandoned for faith in what is unseen and unfelt, where God's seeming absence (to our senses) *is* his presence, and his silence (to our ordinary perception) *is* his speech. It is entering the unknown, letting go of everything familiar we would cling to for security, and discovering that in being "wretchedly and pitiably poor, and blind and naked too" (Rev 3:17) (which grace reveals to us and which we fear to acknowledge—much less accept—in ourselves) lies the potential for all our hope and joy, because to know our true selves is to know we are loved by God beyond all measure.

For the superficial self is an illusion, and must be abandoned on this journey. It is the false self, that strives to possess and hold the sense of the presence of God, which can never be grasped because it is gift, to be received with hands open; it cannot be seized. It is the self which wants to *know* what cannot be known, except in the "unknowing" of intuitive love, the self which struggles to preserve its false existence by defending the illusions which masquerade as its reality: autonomy, control, being the center of its own meaning. And so it is God's compassionate purpose, by means of the darkness we experience in the beginnings of contemplation (and intermittently through our journey into Light) to liberate us from those illusions, which can only bring us disappointment and sorrow.

Perhaps nothing more simple and basic may be said about contemplative prayer than that it is the acceptance of God's invitation not only to trust him in all this, but to *entrust ourselves* to him, so that he may take us beyond ourselves, i.e., beyond our superficial ego-consciousness, which cannot enter upon this mysterious journey into his love.

A rare and beautiful testimony to the way of contemplative prayer is given in the following quotation from a letter of Thomas Merton, written in reply to a Sufi friend who had quite simply asked him how he prayed:

Now you ask about my method of meditation. Strictly speaking I have a very simple way of prayer. It is centered entirely on attention to the presence of God and to his will and his love. That is to say that it is centered on *faith* by which alone we can know the presence of God. One might say this gives my (prayer) the character described by the prophet as "being before God as if you saw him." Yet it does not mean imagining anything or conceiving a precise image of God, for to my mind this would be a kind of idolatry. On the contrary, it is a matter of adoring him as all. . . . There is in my heart this great thirst to recognize totally the nothingness of all that is not God. My prayer is then a kind of praise rising up out of the center of Nothingness and Silence. If I am still present "myself," this I recognize as an obstacle. If he wills he can then make the Nothingness into a total clarity. If he does not will, then the Nothingness actually seems itself to be an object and remains an obstacle. Such is my ordinary way of prayer, or meditation. It is not "thinking about" anything, but a direct seeking of the face of the invisible, which cannot be found unless we become lost in him who is invisible.[8]

Contemplation, writes John of the Cross, "is nothing else than a secret and peaceful and loving inflow of God, which, if not hampered, fires the soul in the spirit of love." But he adds, "The fire of love is not commonly felt at the outset . . . because the soul for want of understanding has not made within itself a peaceful place for it."[9] By continuing to exercise and rely on the intermediaries of our own powers of reflection or will, we will only block that inflow. All that is asked of us is that we "stay quiet before Yahweh, wait longingly for him" (Ps 37:7a).

Here, Jesus' words to the apostles in Gethsemane might well be applied, taken out of context: "Sit here, while *I* pray." Merton provides us with a unique expression of this concept, in saying:

It's a risky thing to pray, and the danger is that our very prayers get between God and us. The great thing in prayer is not to pray, but to go directly to God. If saying your prayers is an obstacle to prayer, cut it out! Let Jesus pray. Thank God Jesus is praying. Forget yourself. Enter into the prayer of Jesus. Let him pray in you. . . . The best way to pray is: stop! Let prayer pray within you, whether you know it or not. This means a deep awareness of our true inner identity . . . (that) by grace we are Christ. Our relationship with God is that of Christ to the Father in the Spirit.[10]

This effacement of self, so that the Spirit of Jesus may pray in us and love in us, is not confined only to times of prayer. As Julian Green said, "One does not have one heart for human beings and another one for God. Therein lies the problem." Gradually learning the blocks we place to his love, and loving enough to remove them (or to allow them to be removed), trusting his love and surrendering to it—all this must find parallels in our daily living, where we slowly learn to choose, over and over again, to give ourselves for others, rather than to get for ourselves.

Quoting Merton again, "Contemplation is out of the question for anyone who doesn't try to cultivate compassion for others." That compassion must extend even—and especially—to ourselves as our darkness is revealed to us, for to deny it or to be angered by it is again the self-perpetuating reaction of the false self.

In books written about saints and mystics, contemplation has so often been associated with extraordinary and sometimes even bizarre phenomena that we probably do not surmise how many true contemplatives we move among, hidden even from themselves. The stereotype of the contemplative as passive, withdrawn, dreamy, and sometimes repressed is a caricature as well, for contemplation requires a capacity for passion, and an ardent love of life. Writing of contemplation, with its sometimes strange terminology (the "dark nights," the aridity of the senses, abandonment, mystical graces, etc.), carries the risk that it may seem unrelated to ordinary life and ordinary people. But *God is "ordinary!"* He has entered our humanity, and he is to be found there, as incarnation reveals, and we and every created thing subsist in him. Writes Elizabeth Barrett Browning:

> Earth's crammed with heaven,
> And every common bush afire with God;
> And only he who sees takes off his shoes;
> The rest sit round it and pluck blackberries.[11]

Further, contemplation is not dependent on a physical cloister (which is by no means a guarantee of producing contemplatives), but on a "cloister of the heart" which, not removed from loving relationships and an active role in the world, becomes the "home" of God, as Jesus promised:

> Anyone who loves me will keep my word,
> and my Father will love him
> and we shall come to him

and make a home in him (Jn 14:23).

To be a contemplative therefore is not limited to any specific life-style, such as monastic or religious; rather, it has everything to do with hearing God's call *to become love,* in whatever state of life we find ourselves. For contemplation will make us not less concerned for the world we live in, but more.

Nevertheless, to grow in this (and any) prayer and to deepen our relationship with God, it is essential that we carve out, every day, some substantial amount of time for interior stillness and silence in prayer, and remain faithful to it as a true priority. Flexibility will be necessary, but it must have as its principle and center our love relationship with God. Lovers do not schedule time to be alone together—they make it happen, knowing that no deep relationship is possible or can endure and grow without it. For "The immanent God may be discovered, but the transcendent God must reveal himself."[12]

Through such faithful commitment to prayer, we will learn that a "passionate waiting," with our hearts awakened and attentive to the One we love, in fidelity and constancy, is of greatest importance, whether we are in light or in darkness. And we will know, as St. Bernard assures us, that "he alone is God who is never sought in vain, even when he cannot be found."[13]

Then, as St. Paul prayed, God himself through his Spirit will enable us to grow in our *inner self,* so that Christ may live in our hearts *through faith,* and, planted in love and built on love, we will have the strength to grasp the breadth and the length, the height and the depth, that *knowing the love of Christ, which is beyond knowing,* we may be filled with the utter fullness of God (Eph 3:16–19). He concludes,

> Glory be to him whose power, working in us, can do infinitely more than we can ask or imagine (v. 20).

Outside times of prayer too, we can learn to "meditate" on life by living reflectively rather than on the surface of things: "listening to life" and recognizing how God is there, as he is in all creation and people and events of our ordinary everyday lives.

To grow in this realization, a very helpful practice is to take some time before the end of each day to reflect and prayerfully discern how God was present and acting, perhaps disguised as commonplace, in moments that passed us by or in circumstances that seemed to conceal rather than reveal him. For the truth is that we are immersed in God, receiving from him life and being and love at every moment, as constantly as the air we breathe throughout our lives. What remains is to open our inner eye and *see* what is always there, to grow in our awareness of this deepest reality, "since it is in him that we live, and move, and exist" (Acts 17:28). As Meister Eckhart humorously commented, "God is always at home. It is we who have gone out for a walk." Contemplation will develop this awareness in developing the gift of faith, which is our participation in God's vision of reality.

Even in small ways there is much we can do to cultivate and nourish an interior life. Since this requires some minimum of interior silence, we can, for example, cut down the constant noise to which we subject ourselves with car radios, TV, etc.; we can choose to avoid useless distractions and commotion, and create for ourselves life-giving islands of quiet and peace. All of this will contribute not only to the quality of our prayer, but to the quality of our relationships, with family and friends and all our contacts with others.

Few of us need look very far for opportunities which challenge our self-centered orientation, that archenemy of spiritual growth, for they abound in any family or group life. In fact, our "guru" may prove to be the very situation we're in, where God is asking us to consent to lay down our lives for others. Many opportunities to die to the false self, in order that the loving life of Christ may rise in us, can be missed when we look for or expect them only in dramatic or heroic occasions. Thérèse of Lisieux said, "Of course we'd like to suffer nobly, in the grand manner . . . what an illusion! To suffer poorly, that's suffering!" "To suffer" means to undergo, to endure, to bear. In this sense there are times when we need go no farther than enduring and bearing with ourselves, with patience and compassion. For to be pitiless or angry with ourselves and our imperfections and failures is only more of the false self's non-acceptance of truth and its illusion of possible perfection. Again, the element of paradox is present in these observations, for every occasion and opportunity to deny the false self is the other side of the coin of freedom and joy. This is Jesus' way, and this is his promise.

Just so, contemplation is ultimately a movement through darkness to light. A rabbinic tale illustrates some implications of this with great sensitivity:

> An ancient rabbi once asked his pupils how they could tell when the night had ended and the day was on its way back. "Could it be," asked one student, "when you can see an animal in the distance and tell whether it is a sheep or a dog?" "No," answered the rabbi. "Could it be," asked another, "when you can look at a tree in the distance and tell whether it is a fig tree or a peach tree?" "No," said the rabbi. "Well, then what is it?" his pupils demanded. "It is when you look on the face of any woman or man and see that she or he is your sister or brother. Because if you cannot do this, then no matter what time it is, it is still night."

To see every woman and every man as sister and brother is to participate in the faith vision of the mystic, whose central intuition is the unity and oneness of ALL, in God. It is a graced effect of contemplation, which gradually transforms our way of seeing reality. This mystical vision is far from an esoteric or "misty" dream, for surely the survival of our planet depends on a universal realization of this unity and the interconnectedness of all peoples and of all the cosmos, in the one Love which is God.

In Karl Rahner's profound statement, "The Christian of the future will be a mystic, or he will not be a Christian at all."

NOTES

1. In the early centuries of the Church, the reading also included the Church Fathers' writings or commentaries on scripture.
2. Jn 14:16–17; 15:26; 16:12–13.
3. Latin: *in* = in; *spirare* = breathe.
4. Scripture Theme #9 (cf Part Two).
5. The Church recapitulates this sending of the Spirit beautifully in

Eucharistic Prayer 4: " . . . that we might live no longer for ourselves but for him, he sent the Holy Spirit from you, Father, as his first gift to those who believe, to complete his work on earth and to bring us the fullness of grace."

6. St Catherine of Siena.

7. *Op. cit.*, p. 146.

8. From Merton's letter to a Sufi scholar, Aziz Ch. Abdul, quoted in Michael Mott's biography, *The Seven Mountains of Thomas Merton* (Boston, MA: Houghton Mifflin Co., 1984), p. 433.

9. *Dark Night,* 10:6, 11:1.

10. *Thomas Merton/Monk, A Monastic Tribute,* ed. by Brother Patrick Hart (Sheed & Ward, Inc., 1974), pp. 88–89. Excerpt is from David Steindl-Rast's chapter, "Man of Prayer."

11. *Aurora Leigh,* Bk vii, 1.821.

12. Carol R. Murphy, *Many Religions: One God* (Pendle Hill, Pa.: Pendle Hill Publications, Pamphlet #150), p. 22.

13. St. Bernard, *On Consideration,* V, XI, 24.

PART TWO

Fifty Scripture Themes for Prayer

Note: On Using the Scripture Themes

In the pages which follow, five hundred different Scripture texts are organized under fifty themes. The *complete* biblical text is indicated by the reference given in the left margin. That text is very briefly summarized in the excerpts given, using only the textual words from the New Jerusalem Bible translation (Doubleday, 1985).

In using these themes for Lectio Divina or any form of prayer, it is suggested that the reader select from the alphabetical list a theme which seems personally appropriate, and then, slowly and prayerfully, proceed to read through the summarized texts until one is found which evokes a personal response. One would then turn to the complete text in the Bible, which will provide the focus for prayer. This may be in accordance with the principles of Lectio Divina, or whatever approach to prayer one is drawn to.

1. Accepting Love

1 Jn 4:7–11 . . . love is from God . . . because God is love . . . it is not we who loved God, but God loved us and sent his Son.

Is 30:18–26 Yahweh is waiting . . . to take pity on you . . . blessed are all who hope in him . . . he will be gracious to you when your cry for help rings out.

Mk 14:3–9 She broke the jar and poured the ointment on his head. Some . . . said . . . "why this waste?" . . . and they were angry with her. But Jesus said, "Leave her alone."

Eph 1:3–13 Blessed be God . . . he chose us in Christ before the world was made . . . marking us out for himself . . . you have been stamped with the seal of the Holy Spirit of the Promise.

Sg 2:8–17 My love lifts up his voice, he says to me, "Come then, my beloved . . . the season of glad songs has come . . . show me your face, let me hear your voice . . . "

Jn 15:9–13 "I have loved you just as the Father has loved me . . . Remain in my love."

Is 54:9–10 I swear never to be angry with you . . . my faithful love will never leave you, my covenant of peace will never totter . . .

Lk 19:41–42 As he drew near the city . . . he shed tears over it and said, "If you had only recognized the way to peace!"

Lk 7:36–50 . . . "her sins, many as they are, have been forgiven her, because she has shown such great love."

Is 43:2–7 Do not be afraid, for I have redeemed you; I have called you by your name, you are mine . . . I am . . . your God . . . I regard you as precious . . . and I love you.

2. The Advent of God

Jas 5:7–11 Now be patient . . . do not lose heart, because the Lord's coming will be soon . . . the Lord is kind and compassionate.

Mt 25:1–13 "The kingdom of Heaven will be like this . . . those who were ready went in with him to the wedding hall and the door was closed . . . So stay awake, because you do not know . . . either the day or the hour."

Is 40:3–5 A voice cries, "Prepare . . . a way for Yahweh, make a straight highway for our God . . . then the glory of Yahweh will be revealed."

Mal 3:1–5 Look, I shall send my messenger to clear a way before me. And suddenly the Lord whom you seek will come to his Temple . . .

1 Thes 5:1–11 . . . the day of the Lord is going to come . . . do not live in the dark, that the Day should take you unawares . . . but stay wide awake . . .

Lk 12:13–21 "Watch, and be on your guard . . . life does not consist in possessions . . . There once was a rich man who . . . thought to himself 'take things easy, eat, drink, and have a good time, . . . instead of becoming rich in the sight of God.

2 Pet 3:3–14 . . . what holy and saintly lives you should be living while you wait for the Day of God to come, and try to hasten its coming . . .

Zec 2:14–17 Sing, rejoice . . . for now I am coming to live among you . . .

Is 56:1–8 . . . act with justice, for soon my salvation will come . . . As for foreigners who adhere to Yahweh I shall make them joyful in my house of prayer.

Heb 10:32–39 Do not lose your fearlessness now . . . only a little while now, a very little while, for come he certainly will before too long.

3. Anxiety

Ps 62:5–8 Rest in God alone, my soul! He is the source of my hope . . .
trust in him . . . pour out your hearts to him . . .

Lam 3:22–26 Surely Yahweh's mercies are not over . . . every morning
they are renewed . . . Yahweh is good to those who trust him, to
all who search for him.

Mt 6:25–34 "I am telling you not to worry about your life . . . Can any
of you . . . add one single cubit to your span of life? . . . will (your
Father) not . . . look after you?"

Ps 142 I pour out my worry in his presence . . . I unfold my troubles
. . . listen to my calling . . . that I may praise your name.

Mk 4:26–29 "This is what the kingdom of God is like . . . night and
day . . . the seed is sprouting and growing . . . how, he does not
know."

Ps 27:10–14 Though my father and mother forsake me, Yahweh will
gather me up . . . be strong, let your heart be bold . . .

Heb 13:5b–9 God himself has said: *I shall not fail you or desert you* . . .

Ps 111 Yahweh is mercy and tenderness . . . he keeps his covenant ever
in mind.

Jos 1:9 . . . go where you may, Yahweh your God is with you.

Ps 43:3–5 Send out your light and your truth; they shall be my guide
. . . Why so downcast, why all these sighs? Hope in God!

4. Beginnings

Rv 22:17 The Spirit and the Bride say, "Come!" Let everyone who listens answer . . .

Mk 1:1–8 Prepare a way for the Lord, make his paths straight . . . he will baptize you with the Holy Spirit.

Jer 8:4–7 Yahweh says . . . if someone falls, can he not stand up again? If people stray, can they not turn back?

Is 65:16–18 . . . past troubles will be forgotten . . . For look, I am going to create new heavens and a new earth, and the past will not be remembered.

Mt 13:44–46 "The kingdom of heaven is like treasure hidden in a field . . . when he finds . . . he goes and sells everything he owns and buys it."

Rv 2:17 . . . to those who prove victorious I will give . . . a white stone with *a new name* written on it . . .

Phl 1:6 . . . the One who began a good work in you will go on completing it . . .

Eph 3:14–21 . . . may he, through his Spirit, enable you to grow so that Christ may live in your hearts . . . that you may be filled with the utter fullness of God.

Is 42:16 I shall lead the blind by a road they do not know . . . I shall turn the darkness into light . . .

Rv 2:1–7 I have this complaint to make: you have less love now than formerly . . . repent, and behave as you did at first . . .

5. The Call of God

Rom 11:29 There is no change of mind on God's part about . . . his choice.

Jn 1:35–39 Jesus . . . saw them following and said, "What do you want?" They answered "where do you live?" He replied, "Come and see" . . .

Dt 7:7–9 Yahweh set his heart on you and chose you . . . the smallest of all . . . because he loved you . . . the faithful God who . . . is true to his covenant . . .

Lk 11:27–28 . . . "blessed are those who hear the word of God and keep it!"

Jer 1:4–10 Before I formed you in the womb I knew you . . . Do not be afraid . . . for I am with you to rescue you . . .

Ps 85:8–9 I am listening. What is God's message?

Jn 8:45–51 . . . "it is because I speak the truth that you do not believe me . . . Whoever comes from God listens to the words of God" . . .

Lk 8:4–15 (Jesus) cried, "Anyone who has ears for listening should listen! . . . people with a noble and generous heart who have heard the word and take it to themselves . . . yield a harvest . . . "

1 Cor 1:2–9 . . . to those . . . called to be God's holy people . . . he will continue to give you strength . . . You can rely on God . . .

Is 6:1–9 I . . . heard the voice of the Lord saying: "Whom shall I send?" . . . And I said, "Here am I, send me."

6. Call to Conversion

Dt 4:29–31 . . . if you search for him honestly and sincerely you will find him . . . For Yahweh your God is a merciful God and will not desert . . . you.

Hos 14:2–10 . . . come back to Yahweh your God . . . Say to him, "Take all guilt away" . . . I shall love them with all my heart . . .

Mk 1:14–15 Jesus went into Galilee . . . saying, "The time is fulfilled . . . Repent, and believe the gospel."

1 Jn 3:4–11 . . . whoever sins has neither seen him nor recognized him . . . whoever does not love his brother is not from God.

Hos 2:16–17 . . . I am going to seduce her and lead her into the desert and speak to her heart.

Jer 24:6–8 My eyes will watch over them . . . to bring them back . . . they will return to me with all their heart.

Jer 31:31–34 I shall make a new covenant . . . Within them I shall plant my Law, writing it on their hearts . . . I shall never more call their sin to mind.

Eph 5:8–14 You were darkness once, but now you are light in the Lord . . . Try to discover what the Lord wants of you . . .

Eph 2:8–10 . . . it is by grace that you have been saved . . . not by anything of your own, but by a gift of God . . . We are God's work of art . . .

Zep 3:14–20 Shout for joy . . . exult with all your heart . . . you have nothing more to fear . . . he will renew you by his love.

7. Children

Mk 10:13–16 People were bringing little children to him . . . Jesus . . . said . . . "it is to such as these that the kingdom of God belongs" . . . Then he embraced them . . .

Mt 18:1–4 . . . the disciples . . . said, "Who is the greatest in the kingdom of heaven?" So he called a little child to him . . .

Mk 9:33–37 . . . they had been arguing which of them was the greatest . . . (Jesus) then took a little child whom he embraced, and he said . . . "Anyone who welcomes a little child . . . welcomes me . . . "

Rom 8:14–17 . . . you received the spirit of adoption, enabling us to cry out "*Abba,* Father!" . . . we are children of God.

1 Jn 3:1–2 . . . what great love the Father has lavished on us by letting us be called God's children—which is what we are.

Ps 131 Yahweh, my heart is not haughty . . . I hold myself in quiet and silence, like a little child in its mother's arms.

Mt 19:13–15 (Jesus said) "Let the little children alone, and do not stop them from coming to me . . . to such as these . . . the kingdom of heaven belongs."

Lk 10:21–22 . . . filled with joy by the Holy Spirit, he said, "I bless you, Father . . . for hiding these things from the learned . . . and revealing them to little children."

Gal 3:25–29 . . . all of you are the children of God, through faith . . . since every one of you that has been baptized has been clothed in Christ.

Lk 16:1–8 For the children of this world are more astute in dealing with their own kind than are the children of light.

8. Compassion

Mk 6:30–44 (Jesus said) "Come away and rest for a while" . . . he saw
a large crowd; and he took pity on them because they were like
sheep without a shepherd . . . "give them something to eat" . . .
Mk 10:46–52 . . . a blind beggar . . . began to shout and cry out . . .
"have pity on me." . . . Jesus stopped and said, "call him here."
(Jesus asked) "what do you want me to do for you?"
Lk 4:38–41 . . . all those who had friends suffering from diseases . . .
brought them to him, and laying his hands on each he cured them.
Ps 34 Yahweh is near to the broken-hearted, he helps those whose spirit
is crushed.
Sir 18:8–14 . . . the Lord is patient . . . Human compassion extends to
neighbors, but the Lord's compassion extends to everyone.
Mt 15:29–39 . . . large crowds came to him, bringing the lame, the crip-
pled, the blind . . . (he) said, "I feel sorry for all these people . . .
I do not want to send them off hungry" . . .
Lk 6:36–37 Be compassionate just as your Father is . . . forgive, and you
will be forgiven.
Is 57:14–19 . . . I am with the contrite and humble, to revive the spirit
. . . I shall heal him . . . fill him with consolation . . . Peace, peace
. . .
Ps 138 I praise your name for your faithful love and your constancy . . .
you gave new strength to my heart.
Neh 9:15–31 . . . because you are a forgiving God, gracious and com-
passionate . . . rich in faithful love, you did not abandon them!

9. *Contrition and Mercy*

1 Pet 2:9–10 . . . you are a chosen race . . . to sing the praises of God who called you out of the darkness . . . now you have received pity.

Jn 12:35–36 Go on your way while you have the light, or darkness will overtake you . . . believe in the light . . .

2 Cor 5:17–6:2 . . . for anyone who is in Christ, there is a new creation . . . It is all God's work . . . we appeal to you to be reconciled to God . . . the day of salvation is here.

Is 54:4–8 Do not fear . . . Yahweh has called you back . . . in great compassion . . . in everlasting love I have taken pity on you.

Jer 3:12–22 Come back . . . since I am merciful . . . I thought: You will call me Father, and will never cease to follow me . . .

Ps 103:1–12 He forgives all your offenses . . . slow to anger and rich in faithful love . . .

Mt 11:28–30 Come to me . . . for I am gentle and humble in heart, and you will find rest . . .

Jn 6:35–39 No one who comes to me will ever hunger; no one who believes in me will ever thirst . . . I will certainly not reject anyone who comes to me.

Is 65:1–2 I have let myself be found by those who did not seek me. I said, "Here I am!"

Ps 130 From the depths I call to you . . . Lord, hear my cry . . . with you is forgiveness . . . my whole being hopes in the Lord . . .

10. *Dialogue of Love with God*

Jer 20:7–13 You have seduced me, Yahweh, and I have let myself be
seduced . . . there seemed to be a fire burning in my heart . . .

Sg 3:1–4 On my bed at night I sought . . . but could not find him . . .
I caught him, would not let him go . . .

Jn 3:16 . . . this is how God loved the world: he gave his only Son . . .

Jn 14:20–21 . . . whoever loves me will be loved by my Father . . . and
I shall . . . reveal myself to him.

Hos 2:21–22 I shall betroth you to myself forever . . . in faithful love
and tenderness.

Jer 31:3 I have loved you with an everlasting love . . .

Jn 15:9–13 I have loved you just as the Father has loved me. Remain in
my love.

Sg 8:6–7 Set me like a seal on your heart . . . for love is strong as Death
. . . Love no flood can quench . . .

Ps 8 I look up at your heavens . . . at the moon and the stars . . . what
are human beings that you spare a thought for them . . . ? yet you
have made (them) little less than a god . . .

Ps 63:1–8 God . . . my heart thirsts for you . . . I will bless you all my
life . . . my heart clings to you.

11. Discernment of Spirits

Lk 7:31–35 "We played the pipes for you, and you wouldn't dance; we sang dirges, and you wouldn't cry."

Col 1:9–14 We . . . ask that through perfect wisdom and spiritual understanding you should reach the fullest knowledge of his will . . .

Mt 6:22–24 " . . . if your eye is clear, your whole body will be filled with light . . . If then, the light inside you is darkened, what darkness that will be!"

Lk 17:20–25 "The coming of the kingdom of God does not admit of observation . . . For look, the kingdom of God is among you."

Rom 12:1–2 . . . let the renewing of your minds transform you so that you may discern for yourselves what is the will of God . . .

Dt 30:15–20 Today . . . I am offering you life or death, blessing or curse. Choose life, then . . .

Eph 4:14–24 Then we shall no longer be . . . tossed one way and another, and carried hither and thither by every new gust of teaching . . . we shall grow completely into Christ.

1 Cor 14:33 . . . God is a God not of disorder but of peace.

1 Cor 12:31—13:3 . . . I put before you the best way of all . . . if I am without love, I am nothing. Though I should give away all that I possess . . . it will do me no good whatever.

Mt 13:10–17 This people's heart has grown coarse, their ears dulled, they . . . avoid using their heart to understand . . . but blessed are your eyes because they see.

12. Discipleship

Col 3:12–15 . . . be clothed in heartfelt compassion . . . bear with one another; forgive each other . . . and may the peace of Christ reign in your hearts . . .

Lk 6:46–49 "Why do you call me, 'Lord, Lord' and not do what I say? Everyone . . . who listens to my words and acts on them—I will show you what such a person is like."

Mt 16:21–26 "If anyone wants to be a follower of mine, let him renounce himself . . . anyone who loses his life for my sake will find it."

Lk 14:7–11 . . . he had noticed how they picked the places of honor . . . "everyone who raises himself up will be humbled . . . "

Gal 2:19–21 . . . it is no longer I, but Christ living in me, . . . who loved me and gave himself for me.

Lk 14:28–33 . . . "which of you, intending to building a tower, would not . . . work out the cost? . . . none of you can be my disciple without giving up all that he owns."

Lk 17:7–10 . . . "when you have done all you have been told to do, say, 'we have done no more than our duty.' "

Ps 127:1–2 If Yahweh does not build a house in vain do its builders toil.

Eph 6:10–20 . . . grow strong in the Lord, with the strength of his power . . . stand your ground, with . . . eagerness to spread the gospel of peace . . .

Jn 13:33–35 " . . . by your love for one another . . . everyone will recognize you as my disciples."

13. Doing Justice

Is 1:11–20 "What are your endless sacrifices to me?" says Yahweh . . . "search for justice . . . be just to the orphan, plead for the widow . . . "

Lk 16:19–31 "There was a rich man who used to . . . feast magnificently every day. And at his gate . . . a poor man who longed to fill himself with what fell from the rich man's table."

Lk 14:12–14 " . . . when you have a party, invite the poor, the crippled, the lame, the blind; then you will be blessed . . . "

Am 5:21–24 I take no pleasure in your solemn assemblies . . . but let justice flow like water, and uprightness like a never-failing stream!

Ex 23:1–9 You will not cheat the poor . . . Do not cause the death of the innocent or upright . . . You will not oppress the alien . . .

Ps 82:1–4 How much longer will you . . . uphold the prestige of the wicked? Let the weak and the orphan have justice, be fair to the wretched and the destitute.

Ex 3:7–8 Yahweh then said, "I have indeed seen the misery of my people . . . I have heard them crying for help on account of their taskmasters."

Jer 22:13–16 . . . your father . . . did what is just and upright . . . he used to examine the cases of the poor and needy . . . Is not that what it means to know me?

Lk 6:20–26 . . . "blessed are you who are poor: the kingdom of God is yours. Blessed are you who are hungry now: you shall have your fill."

Lk 3:10–14 (John the Baptist answered) . . . "Anyone who has two tunics must share with the one who has none, and anyone with something to eat must do the same."

14. *Faith*

Lk 18:1–8 . . . he told them a parable about the need to pray . . . and never lose heart. . . . "But when the Son of man comes, will he find any faith on earth?"

Mt 6:5–8 " . . . pray to your Father who is in that secret place . . . your Father knows what you need before you ask him."

Lk 11:5–13 "Ask, and it will be given to you; search, and you will find; knock, and the door will be opened to you."

Rom 3:21–4:5 . . . God's saving justice given through faith in Jesus Christ to all who believe. No distinction is made.

1 Jn 5:14–15 . . . if we ask anything in accordance with his will he hears us.

Mk 4:35–41 . . . he said to them, "Why are you so frightened? Have you still no faith?" They were overcome with awe.

Is 44:21–24 Remember these things . . . I formed you . . . I shall not forget you.

Jn 14:6–15 "Do you not believe that I am in the Father and the Father is in me? . . . whoever believes in me will perform the same works as I do myself."

Jn 20:24–31 "You believe because you can see me. Blessed are those who have not seen and yet believe."

1 Jn 5:1–11 . . . this is the victory that has overcome the world—our faith.

15. False Self/True Self

Jn 12:24–26 . . . "unless a wheat grain falls into the earth and dies, it remains only a single grain; but if it dies it yields a rich harvest."

2 Cor 5:14–15 . . . those who live should live not any more for themselves, but for him who died and was raised to life.

Rom 7:15–24 . . . though the will to do what is good is in me, the power to do it is not: the good thing I want to do, I never do; the evil thing . . . I do not want—that is what I do.

Lk 22:54–62 . . . a servant-girl saw (Peter) and said, "This man was with him too." But he denied it . . . the Lord turned and looked straight at Peter.

Lk 19:1–10 . . . Zacchaeus said, "I am going to give half my property to the poor . . . " Jesus said to him "Today salvation has come to this house . . . "

Rom 6:3–11 . . . our former self was crucified with him . . . you must see yourselves as being alive for God in Christ Jesus.

Col 3:10–11 You have stripped off your old behavior with your old self, and you have put on a new self . . . renewed in the image of its Creator.

Col 2:11–12 . . . by the complete stripping of your natural self . . . you have been buried with him by your baptism.

Phil 3:7–16 . . . what were once my assets I now through Christ Jesus count as losses . . . if only I can gain Christ.

Mk 8:34–38 "What gain . . . is it for anyone to win the whole world and forfeit his life?"

16. Following the Lord

Lk 5:1–11 . . . Simon Peter fell at the knees of Jesus saying "Leave me, Lord; I am a sinful man." But Jesus said, "Do not be afraid . . . " Then . . . they left everything and followed him.

Mk 2:13–17 . . . (Jesus) saw Levi . . . he said to him, "Follow me." And he got up and followed him. Jesus said . . . "I came to call not the upright, but sinners."

Mt 10:32–42 " . . . if anyone declares himself for me in the presence of human beings, I will declare myself for him in the presence of my Father . . . "

Mt 19:27–30 " . . . everyone who has left houses, (family), or land for the sake of my name will receive a hundred times as much."

Lk 9:57–62 . . . a man . . . said to him, "I will follow you wherever you go." Jesus said . . . "once the hand is laid on the plow, no one who looks back is fit for the kingdom of God."

Ex 13:20–22 Yahweh preceded them . . . to show them the way, and . . . to give them light.

Jer 2:1–13 Yahweh says . . . "I remember your faithful love, the affection of your bridal days . . . my people . . . have abandoned me, the fountain of living water."

Lk 18:18–27 Jesus said, "There is still one thing you lack . . . sell everything . . . distribute the money to the poor . . . then come, follow me."

Jn 21:18–22 " . . . when you were young you . . . walked where you liked; but when you grow old, somebody else will take you where you would rather not go . . . Follow me."

Eph 5:1–2 . . . follow Christ by loving as he loved you, giving himself up for us . . .

17. Forgiveness

Mt 5:43–48 "... love your enemies . . . You must set no bounds to your love, just as your heavenly Father sets none to his."

Lk 23:33–43 . . . they crucified him . . . Jesus said, "Father, forgive them; they do not know what they are doing."

1 Jn 2:3–11 "Whoever claims to be in light but hates his brother is still in darkness . . . not knowing where he is going."

Mt 5:23–26 "... if you . . . remember that your brother has something against you . . . go and be reconciled . . . and then come back . . ."

1 Jn 4:16–21 Let us love, then, because he first loved us . . . whoever does not love his brother whom he can see cannot love God whom he has not seen.

Mt 5:9 "Blessed are the peacemakers . . ."

1 Pet 3:8–12 . . . love the brothers, have compassion and be self-effacing. Never repay one wrong with another . . .

Lk 11:1–4 "... when you pray, this is what to say . . . 'and forgive us our sins, for we ourselves forgive each one who is in debt to us.' "

Mt 18:21–35 Peter said, "Lord, how often must I forgive my brother . . . ?" Jesus answered . . . "seventy-seven times."

Eph 4:25–32 . . . never let the sun set on your anger . . . do not grieve the Holy Spirit . . . Be generous . . . forgiving each other as readily as God forgave you . . .

18. Freedom

Jn 8:31–36 ". . . you will come to know the truth, and the truth will set you free . . . if the Son sets you free, you will indeed be free."

Rom 6:13b–23 . . . you are the slave of him you obey . . . now you are set free from sin and bound to the service of God . . .

Lk 4:16–22 "He has sent me to proclaim liberty to captives, sight to the blind, to let the oppressed go free . . ."

2 Cor 3:12–18 . . . where the Spirit of the Lord is, there is freedom. And all of us are being transformed . . .

Gal 5:16–26 . . . be guided by the Spirit, and you will no longer yield to self-indulgence . . . All who belong to Christ have crucified self . . .

Ps 146 How blessed is he who has . . . God to help him . . . Yahweh sets prisoners free.

Sir 15:11–20 He himself made human beings . . . and then left them free to make their own decisions . . .

Gal 4:1–7 God has sent into our hearts the Spirit of his Son crying, "Abba, Father"; and so you are no longer a slave, but . . . an heir.

Is 45:1–7 I myself shall go before you . . . I shall shatter the bronze gateways . . . give you secret treasures . . . I am Yahweh, who call you by your name.

Is 42:6–9 I have made you a covenant of the people . . . to free captives who live in darkness . . .

19. The Gift of the Holy Spirit

Acts 4:1–31 From this time they were all filled with the Holy Spirit and began to proclaim the word of God fearlessly.

Acts 2:1–13 When Pentecost day came . . . there appeared to them tongues as of fire . . . They were all filled with the Holy Spirit . . .

1 Cor 12:1–13 . . . nobody is able to say, "Jesus is Lord" except in the Holy Spirit. There are many different gifts, but it is always the same Spirit.

Phil 2:1–11 . . . if in Christ there is any fellowship in the Spirit . . . (be) of a single mind, one in love, one in heart and one in mind.

Acts 2:22–47 God raised . . . Jesus to life . . . he has received from the Father the Holy Spirit who was promised and what you see and hear is the outpouring of that Spirit.

Mk 1:1–8 (Jesus) will baptize you with the Holy Spirit.

Jn 6:63–66 "It is the spirit that gives life . . . The words I have spoken to you are spirit and they are life."

Gal 6:7–10 . . . if (someone's) sowing is in the Spirit, then his harvest from the Spirit will be eternal life.

Acts 10:34–48 You know . . . how Jesus of Nazareth began in Galilee . . . God had anointed him with the Holy Spirit.

Rom 8:26–27 . . . the Spirit too comes to help us in our weakness . . . when we do not know how to pray properly . . .

20. God Calls Us To Listen

Jer 7:22–28 . . . when I brought your ancestors out of Egypt, . . . my one command . . . was this: Listen to my voice, then I will be your God and you shall be my people . . . but they did not . . . pay attention.

Dt 6:4–13 Listen, Israel . . . you must love your God with all your heart, with all your soul, with all your strength. Let the words . . . stay in your heart.

Heb 3:7–13 If only you would listen to him today! Do not harden your hearts . . .

Lk 9:28–36 A voice came . . . saying, "This is my Son, the Chosen One. Listen to him."

Mt 7:21–27 "It is not anyone who says to me, 'Lord, Lord,' who will enter the kingdom . . . everyone who listens to these words of mine and does not act on them will be like a stupid man . . . "

Lk 2:19 Mary . . . treasured all these things and pondered them in her heart.

Lk 11:27–28 "More blessed still are those who hear the word of God and keep it!"

Rom 10:5–13 The word is very near to you; it is in your mouth and in your heart, that is, the word of faith . . .

Is 50:4–5 Morning by morning he makes my ear alert to listen like a disciple . . . and I have not resisted.

Jer 7:1–11 Listen to the word of Yahweh . . . amend your behavior . . . treat one another fairly . . . do not exploit the stranger, the orphan and the widow.

21. God in Our Midst

Mt 25:31–46 "Lord, when did we see you hungry and feed you . . . a stranger and make you welcome . . . sick or in prison and go to see you?" " . . . in so far as you did this to one of the least . . . you did it to me."

Mt 26:26–30 . . . as they were eating, Jesus took bread . . . and gave it to the disciples (saying) "this is my body" . . .

Lk 24:13–35 Jesus himself came up and walked by their side; but their eyes were prevented from recognizing him . . .

Col 1:26–29 . . . the message which was a mystery hidden for generations . . . it is Christ among you, your hope of glory.

Jn 14:23 " . . . my Father will love him, and we shall come to him and make a home in him . . . "

1 Cor 6:19–20 . . . the Holy Spirit . . . is in you . . . whom you have received from God . . .

2 Cor 6:16–17 . . . that is what we are—the temple of the living God . . . We have God's word for it . . .

Mt 28:18–20 Jesus . . . spoke to them . . . "look, I am with you always; yes, to the end of time."

Mt 18:19–20 " . . . where two or three meet in my name, I am there among them."

2 Cor 13:3–5 . . . his power is at work among you . . . Do you not recognize yourselves as people in whom Jesus Christ is present?

22. God Reveals Himself to Me

Hos 11:1–4 . . . but they did not know that I was the one caring for them . . . I was like someone lifting an infant to his cheek . . .

Dt 32:3–12 Yahweh . . . your father, who gave you being, who made you, by whom you subsist . . . like an eagle watching its nest, hovering over its young.

Mt 20:1–16 " . . . 'Why should you be envious because I am generous?' Thus the last will be first, and the first, last."

Tit 3:3–8 . . . the kindness and love of God our Savior for mankind were revealed . . . it was for no reason except his own faithful love that he saved us.

Ps 103:13–22 As tenderly as a father treats his children, so Yahweh treats those who fear him . . . (his) faithful love . . . is from eternity and for ever.

Is 49:8–16 Can a woman forget her baby at the breast . . . ? Even if these were to forget, I shall not forget you . . . I have engraved you on the palms of my hands.

Jn 7:37–39 Jesus . . . cried out: "Let anyone who is thirsty come to me!" He was speaking of the Spirit . . .

Mt 9:10–13 . . . the Pharisees . . . said, "Why does your master eat with . . . sinners?" . . . (Jesus) replied, "Go and learn the meaning of the words: 'Mercy is what pleases me, not sacrifice.' "

Mt 21:28–32 (Jesus said) " . . . tax collectors and prostitutes are making their way into the kingdom of God before you."

Jn 17:21–26 "May they all be one . . . Father . . . so that they may also be in us . . . that the world will recognize . . . that you have loved them as you loved me."

23. God's Loving Concern

Ps 145 Yahweh is tenderness and pity, slow to anger, full of faithful love
. . . supports all who stumble . . . lifts up those who are bowed
down . . . close to all who call upon him . . . from the heart.

Jn 4:3–15 Jesus replied . . . "If you only knew what God is offering . . .
no one who drinks the water that I shall give him will ever be
thirsty again."

Rom 8:28–39 . . . God works with those who love him . . . and turns
everything to their good . . . neither death nor life . . . nor any
created thing . . . will ever be able to come between us and the love
of God . . .

Mt 18:12–14 " . . . suppose a man has . . . sheep . . . will he not go in
search of the stray? It is never the will of your Father . . . that one
. . . should be lost."

Is 55 Oh, come to the water all you who are thirsty; though you have
no money, come . . . our God is rich in forgiveness . . .

2 Thes 2:13–17 God chose you from the beginning . . . so that you
should claim as your own the glory of our Lord Jesus Christ.

Lk 15:11–32 (Jesus said) "While he was still a long way off, his father
saw him and was moved with pity. He ran to the boy, clasped him
in his arms and kissed him."

Ps 139 Yahweh . . . you understand my thoughts . . . You created my
inmost self, knit me together in my mother's womb . . . I thank
you; a wonder am I . . . "

Rom 5:1–5 . . . we are at peace with God through our Lord Jesus Christ;
it is through him . . . we have been admitted into God's favor in
which we are living.

Ps 23 Yahweh is my shepherd, I lack nothing . . . He guides me . . .
even were I to walk in a ravine as dark as death I should fear no
danger . . .

24. God's Promises

2 Pet 1:3–11 . . . the greatest and priceless promises have been lavished on us, that through them you should share the divine nature.

Rom 4:16–25 Counting on the promise of God (Abraham) did not doubt or disbelieve . . . fully convinced that whatever God promised he has the power to perform.

2 Cor 1:19–22 Jesus Christ . . . was never Yes-and-No . . . For in him is found the Yes to all God's promises.

Lk 24:44–53 " . . . now I am sending upon you what the Father has promised. Stay in the city, then, until you are clothed with the power from on high."

Eph 3:5–12 . . . the Gentiles now . . . enjoy the same promise in Christ Jesus through the gospel . . . the mystery kept hidden through all the ages in God . . .

1 Jn 2:20–25 . . . no lie can come from the truth . . . and the promise he made you himself is eternal life.

Num 23:19–20 God is no human being that he should lie, no child of Adam to change his mind . . . is it his to speak and not fulfill?

Ez 34:11–16 . . . the Lord . . . says this: Look, I myself shall take care of my flock . . . I shall look for the lost one, bring back the stray, bandage the injured . . . be a true shepherd to them.

Is 46:3–11 Until your old age I shall be the same . . . What I have said, I shall do, what I have planned, I shall perform.

Ez 36:24–28 I shall give you a new heart and put a new spirit in you; I shall remove the heart of stone from your bodies and give you a heart of flesh . . .

25. Gratitude

Mk 5:18–20 Jesus said . . . "Go home to your people and tell them all that the Lord in his mercy has done for you."

Lk 17:11–19 They . . . called to him, "Jesus! Master! Take pity on us" . . . they were cleansed . . . one of them . . . thanked him . . . This led Jesus to say, "Were not all ten made clean? The other nine, where are they?"

Col 3:16–17 Let the Word of Christ . . . find a home with you . . . With gratitude in your hearts sing . . . songs to God.

Ps 116 I am filled with love when Yahweh . . . bends down to hear me . . . What return can I make . . . for his generosity to me?

Ps 104 I shall sing to Yahweh all my life, make music for my God as long as I live . . . for Yahweh gives me joy.

Eph 5:15–20 Make the best of the present time . . . be filled with the Spirit . . . always and everywhere giving thanks to God.

Col 2:2–10 . . . as you received Jesus as Lord . . . now live your lives in him, rooted in him . . . and overflowing with thanksgiving.

Ps 50:8–15 Let thanksgiving be your sacrifice to God, fulfill the vows you make . . . then you will honor me.

Ps 100 . . . come into his presence with songs of joy! give thanks to him and bless his name!

Ps 65 Praise is rightfully yours, God . . . Our faults overwhelm us, but you blot them out . . . hope of the whole wide world . . .

26. Hearing God's Word

Mk 4:1–20 "Anyone who has ears for listening should listen . . . hear the word and accept it and yield a harvest . . . "

Mt 17:1–8 . . . there came a voice . . . "This is my Son, the Beloved . . . Listen to him." Jesus touched them, saying, " . . . do not be afraid."

Lk 10:38–42 Mary . . . sat down at the Lord's feet and listened to him speaking . . . Martha . . . came to him and said, "Please tell her to help me."

Jn 10:27–30 "The sheep that belong to me listen to my voice . . . I give them eternal life; they will never be lost."

Lk 10:23–24 " . . . many prophets and kings wanted to . . . hear what you hear, and never heard it."

Ps 37:3–7 Stay quiet before Yahweh, wait longingly for him.

Jn 5:36–47 " . . . the Father has sent me . . . You have never heard his voice . . . and his word finds no home in you because you do not believe."

Rom 10:14–21 . . . how can they believe in him if they have never heard of him? . . . faith comes from hearing, and that means hearing the word of Christ.

Is 43:1–2 Do not be afraid, for I have redeemed you; I have called you by your name, you are mine.

Rv 3:13–22 " . . . Look, I am standing at the door, knocking. If one of you hears me calling and opens the door, I will come in . . . "

27. *Joy*

Jn 3:28–30 This is the joy I feel, and it is complete. He must grow greater, I must grow less.

Jn 16:20–24 " . . . you will be sorrowful, but your sorrow will turn to joy . . . and that joy no one shall take from you."

Lk 24:36–43 . . . he himself stood among them and said to them: "Peace be with you!" . . . Their joy was so great that they still could not believe it.

1 Pet 1:3–9 You have not seen him, yet you love him . . . already filled with a joy so glorious that it cannot be described.

Lk 24:50–53 They worshipped him and then went back to Jerusalem full of joy.

1 Jn 1:1–5 Something which we have heard, which we have seen . . . and touched with our own hands, the Word of life . . . we are declaring to you . . . so that our joy may be complete.

Lk 1:40–55 My soul proclaims the greatness of the Lord and my spirit rejoices in God my Savior.

Ps 84 My heart and my body cry out for joy to the living God . . . How blessed are those . . . who find their strength in you.

Rv 19:5–9 Alleluia! The reign of the Lord our God Almighty has begun; let us be glad and joyful . . .

Rom 14:17–19 . . . it is not eating and drinking that make the kingdom of God, but the saving justice, the peace and the joy brought by the Holy Spirit.

28. The Kingdom and the Poor

Dt 8:11–20 When you have eaten all you want . . . have seen your silver and gold abound and all your possessions grow great . . . do not then forget your God.

Mk 10:17–27 "How hard it is for those who have riches to enter the kingdom of God . . . but . . . for God everything is possible."

Lk 14:15–24 "When the time for the banquet came . . . all alike started to make excuses . . . the householder said, 'Go out quickly into the streets . . . and bring in here the poor, the crippled, the blind and the lame.' "

Dt 24:12–22 You must not exploit a poor and needy wage-earner . . . you must not infringe the rights of the foreigner or the orphan.

Ps 37:8–17 Though the wicked draw his sword . . . and bring down the poor and the needy, his sword will pierce his own heart.

Jas 2:12–17 . . . if good deeds do not go with (faith), it is quite dead.

Mk 12:41–44 He . . . watched the people putting money into the treasury . . . the rich put in a great deal. A poor widow put in . . . a penny. Then he said "this poor widow has put more in than all."

Ps 41:1–3 Blessed is anyone who cares for the poor and the weak; in time of trouble Yahweh rescues him.

Dt 10:14–21 (Yahweh) it is who sees justice done . . . who loves the stranger and gives him food and clothing. (Love the stranger then, for you were once strangers . . .)

Acts 20:28–36 . . . we must exert ourselves . . . to support the weak, remembering the words of the Lord Jesus . . . "There is more happiness in giving than in receiving."

29. Learning from Jesus (A)

Mt 13:31–32 "The kingdom of heaven is like a mustard seed . . . the smallest of all . . . but . . . when grown it . . . becomes a tree."

Jn 2:13–25 . . . in the Temple he found people selling . . . and the money changers sitting there . . . he drove them all out . . . knocked their tables over and said, " . . . stop using my Father's house as a market."

Jn 15:14–17 "I call you friends . . . you did not choose me, no, I chose you."

Lk 17:7–10 " . . . when you have done all you have been told to do, say . . . 'we have done no more than our duty.' "

Mt 12:15–21 Look . . . my beloved, in whom my soul delights . . . he will not break the crushed reed, or snuff the faltering wick . . .

Mt 7:12–20 " . . . always treat others as you would like them to treat you . . . Enter by the narrow gate . . . that leads to life, and only a few find it."

Jn 7:14–18 "My teaching is not from myself; it comes from the one who sent me; anyone who is prepared to do his will, will know whether my teaching is from God."

Mk 2:1–12 Seeing their faith, Jesus said to the paralytic, " . . . your sins are forgiven." . . . they were all astonished and praised God . . .

Jn 21:1–14 . . . there stood Jesus on the shore . . . there was some bread there and a charcoal fire with fish . . . Jesus said . . . "Come and have breakfast."

Mt 13:24–30 "The kingdom of heaven may be compared to a man who sowed good seed . . . his enemy sowed darnel all among the wheat . . . the laborers said, 'Do you want us to go and weed it out?' "

30. *Learning from Jesus (B)*

Jn 8:1–11 "Let the one among you who is guiltless be the first to throw a stone at her." . . . When they heard this they went away one by one.

Mt 15:21–28 . . . a Canaanite woman . . . started shouting . . . "take pity on me." . . . he said not a word in answer . . . "Lord," she said, "help me." Jesus answered . . . "Woman, you have great faith. Let your desire be granted."

Mt 22:34–40 " . . . love the Lord your God with all your heart . . . love your neighbor as yourself. On these two commandments hang the whole Law . . . "

Lk 9:1–6 . . . he sent them out to proclaim the kingdom of God and to heal . . . "Take nothing for the journey" . . . So they set out . . . proclaiming the good news.

Jn 3:17–21 " . . . though the light has come into the world people have preferred darkness . . . but whoever does the truth comes out into the light."

Jn 20:11–20 . . . Mary was standing outside near the tomb, weeping . . . Jesus said to her, "Woman, why are you weeping? Whom are you looking for?"

Mt 26:47–56 (Judas) went up to Jesus . . . and kissed him. Jesus said to him, "My friend . . . " . . . all the disciples deserted him and ran away.

Mk 13:33–37 "Be on your guard . . . stay awake, because you do not know when the master . . . is coming . . . he must not find you asleep."

Lk 7:1–10 . . . the centurion sent word . . . to say to him, "I am not worthy to have you under my roof . . . let my boy be cured by your giving the word." Jesus . . . was astonished.

Jn 5:1–20 " . . . by himself the Son can do nothing; he can only do what he sees the Father doing."

31. Learning from Jesus (C)

Jn 4:21–26 "God is spirit, and those who worship must worship in spirit and truth" . . . The woman said, "I know that . . . Christ is coming" . . . Jesus said, "That is who I am."

Mt 12:46–50 . . . stretching out his hand toward his disciples he said, "Here are my mother and my brothers. Anyone who does the will of my Father . . . "

Mt 21:28–32 "What is your opinion? A man had two sons . . . which of the two did his father's will?"

Lk 9:18–22 "But you," he said to them, "who do you say I am?"

Mk 9:2–9 Jesus . . . led them up a high mountain . . . There in their presence he was transfigured . . . (Peter) said, "it is wonderful to be here; so let us make three shelters" . . .

Jn 8:12 " . . . anyone who follows me will not be walking in the dark but will have the light of life."

Mk 12:28–34 "Which is the first of all the commandments?" Jesus replied, " . . . you must love the Lord your God . . . You must love your neighbor as yourself."

Jn 6:14–15 Jesus, as he realized they were about to . . . make him king, fled back to the hills alone.

Jn 12:44–50 " . . . whoever sees me, sees the one who sent me. I have come . . . to prevent anyone who believes in me from staying in the dark any more."

Jn 21:15–17 Jesus said to Simon Peter . . . a third time . . . "do you love me? . . . Feed my sheep."

32. Lent

Lk 5:27–39 Jesus said . . . "I have come to call not the upright but sinners to repentance."

1 Jn 1:6–10 If we say "we have no sin," we are deceiving ourselves . . . he will forgive our sins and will cleanse us from all evil.

Jl 2:12–14 "But now"—declares Yahweh—"come back to me with all your heart" . . . he is gracious and compassionate, slow to anger, rich in faithful love.

Is 58:1–12 Is this not the sort of fast that pleases me: to break unjust fetters . . . sharing your food with the hungry and sheltering the homeless poor.

Ps 51 Have mercy on me, O God, in your faithful love . . . create in me a clean heart, renew within me a resolute spirit.

Lk 9:23–26 "Anyone who wants to save his life will lose it; but anyone who loses his life for my sake will save it."

Ps 40 You wanted no sacrifice . . . but you gave me an open ear . . . your law, my God, is deep in my heart . . . Poor and needy as I am, the Lord has me in mind.

Is 42:1–4 Here is my servant whom I uphold, my chosen one in whom my soul delights . . . he will bring fair judgment . . .

Jb 19:25–27a . . . he will set me close to him, and from my flesh I shall look on God.

Ps 42 As a deer yearns for running streams, so I yearn for you, my God . . . Why be so downcast, why all these sighs? Hope in God!

33. *Life Everlasting*

Jn 17:1–3 " . . . eternal life is this: to know you, the only true God, and Jesus Christ whom you have sent."

Jn 5:21–30 " . . . whoever listens to my words, and believes in the one who sent me, has eternal life . . . such a person has passed from death to life."

Jn 11:25–26 "I am the resurrection. Anyone who believes in me, even though that person dies, will live."

1 Cor 15:49–57 . . . And as we have borne the likeness of the earthly man, so we shall bear the likeness of the heavenly one.

Rv 21:1–7 He will wipe away all tears from their eyes; there will be no more death, no more mourning or sadness or pain.

Jn 14:1–3 "I am going to prepare a place for you, and after . . . I shall return to take you to myself so that you may be with me."

2 Tm 2:10–13 If we have died with him, then we shall live with him . . . If we are faithless, he is faithful still.

Jn 6:67–69 Lord, to whom shall we go? You have the message of eternal life.

1 Jn 5:12–13 Whoever has the Son has life . . .

2 Cor 4:13–15 . . . he who raised up the Lord Jesus will raise us up with Jesus in our turn, and bring us to himself.

34. *The Life-Giving Spirit*

Lk 1:26–38 The Holy Spirit will come upon you, and the power of the Most High will cover you . . . And so the child . . . will be called Son of God.

Jn 14:25–26 " . . . the Holy Spirit, whom the Father will send in my name, will teach you everything."

Acts 9:10–19 Ananias . . . laid his hands on Saul and said, "Brother Saul, I have been sent by the Lord Jesus, so that you may . . . be filled with the Holy Spirit."

Acts 8:26–39 The Spirit said to Philip, "Go up and join that chariot" . . . he heard him reading Isaiah the prophet . . . Philip proceeded to explain the good news of Jesus to him.

1 Jn 4:12–15 This is the proof that we remain in him and he in us, that he has given us a share in his Spirit.

Eph 2:17–22 Through (Jesus) . . . we both in the one Spirit have free access to the Father.

Acts 1:1–8 " . . . you will receive the power of the Holy Spirit which will come on you, and then you will be my witnesses . . ."

Ez 37:1–14 The Lord Yahweh says this . . . "I am now going to make breath enter you, and you will live . . . you will know that I am Yahweh, when I . . . put my spirit in you."

Jl 3:1–2 "I shall pour out my spirit on all humanity . . . "

Jn 3:3–8 " . . . no one can enter the kingdom of God without being born through water and the Spirit . . . what is born of the Spirit is spirit."

35. Newness of Life: The Easter Mystery

Rom 7:4–6 . . . you are able to belong to . . . him who was raised from the dead to make us live fruitfully for God . . . having died to what was binding us.

Eph 2:1–7 God . . . through the great love with which he loved us, even when we were dead in our sins, brought us to life with Christ.

2 Cor 5:1–9 . . . so that what is mortal in us may be swallowed up by life . . . It is God who . . . has given us the Spirit as a pledge.

Rv 1:4–8 Jesus Christ . . . the First-born from the dead . . . loves us and has washed away our sins.

Lk 7:18–23 " . . . the blind see again, the lame walk . . . the dead are raised to life . . . blessed is anyone who does not find me a cause of falling."

Acts 17:22–34 . . . it is he who gives everything—including life and breath—to everyone . . . it is in him that we live, and move, and exist.

1 Pet 2:21–25 He was bearing our sins in his own body on the cross, so that we might die to our sins and live for uprightness . . .

Rom 1:3–7 (Jesus) in terms of the Spirit . . . was designated Son of God in power by resurrection from the dead, Jesus Christ our Lord through whom we have received grace and our apostolic mission . . . by his call you belong to Jesus Christ.

2 Cor 4:7–12 . . . we hold this treasure in pots of earthenware, so that the immensity of the power is God's and not our own . . . so that the life of Jesus . . . may be visible in our mortal flesh.

Rom 5:6–11 . . . it is proof of God's love for us, that Christ died for us while we were still sinners . . . through him we have . . . gained our reconciliation.

36. *Peace and Confidence*

Jn 14:27–29 ". . . my own peace I give you . . . which the world cannot give . . . Do not let your hearts be troubled or afraid."

Jn 16:25–33 ". . . the Father himself loves you for loving me . . . I have told you all this so that you may find peace in me."

Heb 10:14–24 . . . the Lord says . . . I shall never more call their sins to mind . . . the one who made the promise is trustworthy.

Lk 12:22–32 "I am telling you not to worry about your life . . . there is no need to be afraid . . . for it has pleased your Father to give you the kingdom."

Ps 52:8–9 But I . . . put my trust in God's faithful love . . . I shall praise you forever for what you have done.

Is 9:5–6 . . . a son has been born for us . . . to extend his dominion in boundless peace.

Jas 3:13–18 . . . the wisdom that comes down from above is peaceable, kindly and considerate . . . The peace sown by peacemakers brings a harvest of justice.

Is 40:28–30 Yahweh is the everlasting God . . . his understanding is beyond fathoming. He gives strength to the weary.

Ps 4 Yahweh listens when I call to him . . . In peace I lie down and at once fall asleep . . . it is you . . . who make me rest secure.

Heb 7:25–27 . . . his power to save those who come to God through him is absolute . . . he lives forever to intercede for them.

37. Prayer in Scripture

Jas 5:13–20 Any one of you who is in trouble should pray . . . the heartfelt prayer of someone upright works very powerfully.

Lk 6:12–13 (Jesus) went onto the mountain to pray; and he spent the whole night in prayer to God.

Mt 26:36–44 Jesus came with them to . . . Gethsemane . . . and said, "Stay here while I go over there to pray . . . " going on a little further he fell on his face and prayed.

Lk 22:39–46 He . . . knelt down and prayed. "Father . . . your will be done, not mine" . . . and his sweat fell to the ground like great drops of blood.

Mk 11:24–25 (Jesus said) " . . . when you stand in prayer, forgive whatever you have against anybody."

Ps 95:1–7 Let us come into his presence with thanksgiving . . . let us bow low and do reverence; kneel before Yahweh who made us!

Ps 100 Acclaim Yahweh . . . come into his presence with songs of joy . . . give thanks to him and bless his name!

1 Tm 2:1–8 I urge . . . that petitions, prayers, intercessions and thanksgiving should be offered for everyone . . . so that we may be able to live peaceful and quiet lives.

Phil 4:4–9 The Lord is near . . . tell God all your desires . . . in prayer . . . shot through with gratitude, and the peace of God . . . will guard your hearts and thoughts.

Mt 6:5–8 " . . . when you pray, do not imitate the hypocrites: they love to say their prayers . . . for people to see them . . . pray to your Father who is in that secret place."

38. *Reconciliation*

Mt 6:9–15 "Our Father . . . your kingdom come . . . forgive us . . . as we have forgiven . . . "

Eph 2:12–16 . . . now in Christ Jesus, you that used to be so far off have been brought close . . . For he is the peace between us.

Jn 20:19–23 He said to them, "Peace be with you . . . Receive the Holy Spirit. If you forgive anyone's sins they are forgiven."

1 Cor 13:4–7 Love is always patient . . . it does not take offense or store up grievances . . . It is always ready to make allowances . . .

Gn 45:1–15 Joseph made himself known to his brothers, but he wept . . . Then he said, "Come closer to me . . . do not reproach yourselves for having sold me here" . . . He kissed all his brothers, weeping on each one.

Si 28:1–7 If anyone nurses anger against another, can one then demand compassion from the Lord?

Wis 12:19–22 (Yahweh,) you instruct us . . . that we should reflect on your kindness when we judge, and, when we are judged, we should look for mercy.

Lk 17:3–4 "If he wrongs you seven times a day . . . and says, 'I am sorry,' you must forgive him."

Ps 32 How blessed are those whose offense is forgiven . . . one who trusts in Yahweh is enfolded in his faithful love.

1 Jn 1:6–10 If we say that we share in God's life while we are living in darkness . . . we are not living the truth . . . he will forgive our sins and will cleanse us . . .

39. Relationships

Lk 9:46–50 An argument started between them about which of them was the greatest. Jesus . . . said to them, "The least among you all is the one who is the greatest."

Jas 2:1–8 . . . do not let class distinction enter into your faith in Jesus . . . the right thing to do is to keep the supreme Law of scripture: *you will love your neighbor as yourself.*

Mt 12:46–50 . . . stretching out his hand toward his disciples he said . . . "Anyone who does the will of my Father is my brother and sister and mother."

1 Pet 1:22–2:1 . . . love each other intensely from the heart . . . Rid yourselves . . . of all spite, deceit, hypocrisy, envy and carping criticism.

Lk 6:36–38 Be compassionate just as your Father is compassionate . . . do not judge . . . do not condemn . . . forgive . . .

Lk 10:29–37 . . . the man said . . . "who is my neighbor?" Jesus said, "A man . . . fell into the hands of bandits . . . a Samaritan traveller who came on him was moved with compassion . . . which, do you think, proved himself a neighbor . . . ?"

1 Cor 10:16–17 . . . we, although there are many of us, are one single body, for we all share in the one loaf.

Mt 20:24–28 " . . . anyone who wants to become great among you must be your servant . . . just as the Son of man came not to be served but to serve."

Eph 4:1–6 . . . support each other in love . . . preserve the unity of the Spirit by the peace that binds you together.

Mt 7:1–5 "Do not judge, and you will not be judged . . . how dare you say to your brother, 'Let me take that splinter out of your eye,' when, look, there is a great log in your own?"

40. Security in God

Jn 10:9–15 "I am the gate. Anyone who enters through me will be safe
. . . I am the good shepherd . . . and I lay down my life for my
sheep."

Mt 18:12–14 "Suppose a man has a hundred sheep . . . will he not . . .
go in search of the stray? . . . Similarly, it is never the will of your
Father that one . . . should be lost."

Mt 6:19–21 " . . . store up treasures for yourselves in heaven, where
. . . thieves cannot break in and steal."

Ps 27 Yahweh is my light and my salvation, whom should I fear? . . .
Though my father and mother forsake me Yahweh will gather me
up.

Is 41:8–13 I have chosen you, I have not rejected you, do not be afraid,
for I am with you . . . I shall help you.

Jer 29:11–14 I know what plans I have in mind for you . . . plans for
peace, not for disaster, to give you a future and a hope.

Jdt 9:11–12 . . . you are the God of the humble, the help of the oppressed, the support of the weak . . . the Savior of the despairing.

Ps 86 Listen to me, Yahweh, answer me . . . save your servant who
relies on you . . . you are kind and forgiving, rich in faithful love
for all who call upon you.

Ps 91 Since he clings to me I rescue him, I raise him high, since he ac-
knowledges my name. He calls to me and I answer him: in distress
I am at his side.

Is 25:4–9 You are my God . . . you have been a refuge . . . for the needy
in distress, a shelter from the storm . . . Yahweh has wiped away
the tears from every cheek . . . we put our hope in him.

41. Seeking God

Jn 6:44–47 No one can come to me unless drawn by the Father who sent me.

Ps 73:23–28 . . . you will draw me in the wake of your glory. Who else is there for me in heaven? . . . My heart and my flesh are pining away . . . my happiness is to be near God.

Col 3:1–4 . . . you must look for the things that are above . . . now the life you have is hidden with Christ in God . . . and he is your life.

Is 65:24 I have let myself be found by those who did not seek me. I said, "Here I am!" . . . Each day I stretched out my hands . . .

Jn 1:35–39 Jesus . . . saw them following and said, "What do you want?" They answered, "Where do you live?" He replied, "Come and see."

Ps 143:5–10 I stretch out my hands to you, my heart like a land thirsty for you . . . Let dawn bring news of your faithful love, for I place my trust in you.

Dn 3:39–42 And now we put our whole heart into following you . . . seeking your face once more. Do not abandon us . . .

2 Chr 15:12–15 They . . . made a covenant to seek Yahweh . . . with all their heart and soul . . . and sought him so earnestly that he allowed them to find him.

Ps 105:1–5 . . . let the hearts that seek Yahweh rejoice! tirelessly seek his presence!

Ps 24:1–6 Who shall go up to the mountains of Yahweh? . . . The clean of hands and pure of heart, whose heart is not set on vanities.

42. Service

Lk 22:24–27 " . . . the greatest among you must behave as if he were the youngest . . . here am I among you as one who serves!"

Mt 23:1–12 Anyone who raises himself up will be humbled, and anyone who humbles himself will be raised up.

Lk 17:7–10 " . . . when you have done all you have been told to do, say . . . 'we have done no more than our duty.' "

Mt 24:42–51 "Who, then, is the wise and trustworthy servant? But if the servant . . . says to himself, 'My master is taking his time' . . . his master will come on a day he does not expect."

Eph 4:11–13 . . . (Jesus') gift was . . . to knit God's holy people together for the work of service to build up the Body of Christ . . .

2 Cor 4:5–7 It is not ourselves that we are proclaiming, but Christ Jesus as the Lord, and ourselves as your servants for Jesus' sake.

Col 3:23–25 Whatever your work is, put your heart into it . . . It is Christ the Lord that you are serving.

Gal 5:13–15 . . . you were called to be free . . . be servants to one another in love . . .

Rom 12:3–13 In the service of the Lord, work not half-heartedly but with . . . an eager spirit . . . look for opportunities to be hospitable.

Jn 13:1–20 Jesus . . . began to wash the disciples' feet . . . When he went back to the table . . . "Do you understand," he said, "what I have done to you? . . . I have given you an example."

43. The Spirit of God

Jn 14:16–19 "I shall ask the Father and he will give you another Paraclete to be with you for ever, the Spirit of truth . . . he is with you, he is in you."

Jas 4:1–10 The longing of the spirit he sent to dwell in us is a jealous longing . . .

Rom 8:9–13 . . . the Spirit of God has made a home in you. Indeed, anyone who does not have the Spirit of Christ does not belong to him.

1 Cor 3:16–23 Do you not realize that you are a temple of God with the Spirit of God living in you?

1 Cor 2:9–16 . . . The Spirit we have received is . . . God's own Spirit, so that we may understand the lavish gifts God has given us.

1 Thes 5:19–24 Do not stifle the Spirit . . . May the God of peace make you perfect and holy . . . He who has called you . . . will carry it out.

Eph 1:13–14 . . . you have been stamped with the seal of the Holy Spirit of the Promise . . . for the praise of his glory.

Rom 8:18–25 . . . we too, who have the first fruits of the Spirit . . . are . . . waiting with eagerness for our bodies to be set free.

2 Tm 1:6–14 . . . fan into a flame the gift of God that you possess . . . (God gave us) the Spirit of power and love and self-control.

Jn 16:12–15 "I still have many things to say to you . . . However, when the Spirit of truth comes he will lead you to the complete truth."

44. Stewardship

Mt 25:14–30 "It is like a man . . . who summoned his servants and entrusted his property to them . . . he gave . . . each in proportion to his ability . . . to everyone who has will be given more . . . anyone who has not will be deprived even of what he has."

Lk 12:42–48 "Who . . . is the wise and trustworthy steward whom the master will place over his household . . . ? When someone is entrusted with a great deal, of that person even more will be expected."

1 Cor 4:1–7 People should think of us as . . . stewards entrusted with the mysteries of God . . . each one should be found trustworthy.

Jn 1:15–18 Indeed, from his fullness we have, all of us, received—one gift replacing another.

2 Cor 9:6–11 . . . anyone who sows sparsely will reap sparsely . . .

Lk 6:38 Give, and there will be gifts for you . . . the standard you use will be the standard used for you.

Mk 4:21–25 " . . . is a lamp . . . to be put under a tub or under a bed? Surely to be put on the lamp-stand?"

1 Cor 3:5–9 . . . each has only what the Lord has given him . . .

1 Pet 4:8–11 Each one of you has received a special grace, so, like good stewards . . . put it at the service of others.

1 Cor 9:14–27 I am simply accepting a task entrusted to me . . . this I do for the sake of the gospel, that I may share its benefits with others.

45. Suffering

Rv 7:13–17 They will never hunger or thirst again . . . because the Lamb . . . will be their shepherd and will guide them to springs of living water.

Heb 2:9–18 For the suffering he himself passed through enables him to help others when they are being put to the test.

2 Cor 4:16–18 . . . though this outer human nature of ours may be falling into decay . . . our inner human nature is renewed day by day . . .

Is 53:2–7 . . . ours were the sufferings he was bearing . . . he was being wounded for our rebellions . . . the punishment reconciling us fell on him.

Mk 14:32–42 They came to Gethsemane . . . he began to feel terror and anguish. And he said to them . . . "stay awake . . . The spirit is willing enough, but human nature is weak."

2 Tm 2:1–9 . . . take strength from the grace which is in Christ Jesus . . . Bear with your share of difficulties . . . the Lord will give you full understanding.

Ps 30 I cried to you for help and you healed me . . . In the evening come tears, but with dawn cries of joy . . . You have turned my mourning into dancing.

2 Cor 1:3–7 . . . God who gives every possible encouragement; he supports us in every hardship, so that we are able to come to the support of others.

Gn 50:18–21 . . . is it for me to put myself in God's place? The evil you planned to do me has by God's design been turned to good.

Is 25:4–9 . . . you have been a refuge for the needy in distress, a shelter from the storm . . . Yahweh has wiped away the tears from every cheek.

46. The Tenderness of God

Lk 7:11–17 . . . he went to a town called Nain . . . there was a dead man being carried out, the only son of his mother . . . the Lord . . . felt sorry for her and said to her, "Don't cry."

Mt 20:29–34 . . . they shouted, "Lord! Have pity on us" . . . Jesus stopped, called them over and said, "What do you want me to do for you?"

Is 40:9–11 He is like a shepherd . . . gathering lambs in his arms, holding them against his breast . . .

Mt 23:37–39 "How often have I longed to gather your children together, as a hen gathers her chicks under her wings . . . "

Mk 1:39–41 A man suffering . . . came to him and pleaded on his knees . . . Feeling sorry for him, Jesus . . . touched him . . .

Ps 25:1–10 . . . he guides the humble . . . kindness unfailing and constancy mark all Yahweh's paths . . .

Lk 15:1–7 "I tell you, there will be more rejoicing in heaven over one sinner repenting than over ninety-nine . . . who have no need of repentance."

Jn 11:32–44 At the sight of (Mary's) tears . . . Jesus was greatly distressed . . . Jesus wept, and the Jews said, "See how much he loved him!"

Is 61:1–8 Yahweh . . . has sent me . . . to soothe the broken-hearted . . . to comfort all who mourn.

Ps 103:13–22 As tenderly as a father treats his children, so Yahweh treats those who fear him . . . he remembers that we are dust . . . But Yahweh's faithful love . . . is from eternity and forever . . .

47. *Trust*

Lk 8:40–56 Jesus said, "Do not be afraid, only have faith" . . . They were all crying and mourning for her, but Jesus said, "Stop crying; she is not dead but asleep."

Mt 9:27–31 . . . he said to them, "Do you believe I can do this?" They said, "Lord, we do."

2 Kgs 5:1–16 Elisha sent him a messenger to say "go and bathe . . . in the Jordan, and your flesh will become clean . . . " But Naaman . . . went off in a rage. " . . . if the prophet had asked you to do something difficult, would you not have done it?"

Ps 56 When I am afraid, I put my trust in you . . . and have no fear, what can mortal man do to me?

1 Tm 1:12–17 Jesus Christ meant to make me the leading example of his inexhaustible patience for all . . . who were later to trust in him . . .

Mk 6:1–6 . . . he went to his home town and . . . began teaching . . . And they would not accept him . . . He was amazed at their lack of faith.

Ps 125 Whoever trusts in Yahweh is like Mount Zion: unshakeable, it stands forever . . . Yahweh encircles his people, henceforth and for ever.

Jas 1:2–18 . . . a person who has doubts is like the waves . . . Blessed is anyone who perseveres when trials come . . . Never . . . say, "God is tempting me."

1 Pet 5:6–11 . . . the God of all grace . . . will confirm, strengthen and support you. His power lasts for ever . . .

Is 26:1–9 Trust in Yahweh for ever, for Yahweh is a rock for ever . . .

48. Truth and Integrity

Mt 15:1–20 " 'This people honors me only with lip-service, while their hearts are far from me. Their reverence of me is worthless.' "

Mk 3:1–5 "Is it permitted on the Sabbath day to do good, or to do evil; to save life, or to kill?"

Lk 6:43–45 "There is no sound tree that produces rotten fruit . . . the words of the mouth flow out of what fills the heart."

Mt 23:13–32 " . . . from the outside you look upright, but inside you are full of hypocrisy . . . "

Lk 13:10–17 . . . the president of the synagogue was indignant because Jesus had healed on the Sabbath . . . the Lord said, "Hypocrites . . . "

Jn 15:1–10 "Whoever remains in me, with me in him, bears fruit in plenty . . . cut off from me you can do nothing."

1 Jn 3:14–19 . . . our love must be not just words or mere talk, but something active and genuine.

Rom 12:14–21 Pay no regard to social standing, but meet humble people on their own terms.

Jn 18:33–40 "I was born for this . . . to bear witness to the truth; and all who are on the side of truth listen to my voice."

Mt 22:15–22 Jesus replied, "You hypocrites! Why are you putting me to the test? . . . pay Caesar what belongs to Caesar—and God what belongs to God."

49. Weakness and Strength

1 Cor 1:25–31 God's weakness is stronger than human strength . . . He
chose those who . . . are weak to shame the strong . . . indeed
those who count for nothing.

2 Cor 12:7–10 . . . but he has answered me, "My grace is enough for
you: for power is at full strength in weakness."

Lk 18:9–14 He spoke . . . to some people who prided themselves on
being upright and despised everyone else . . .

Heb 5:7–9 (Jesus) offered up prayer and entreaty, with loud cries and
with tears . . .

Ps 16 Yahweh, you, you alone, hold my lot secure . . . with him . . .
nothing can shake me.

Acts 3:11–16 . . . why are you so surprised at this? . . . as though we
had made this man walk by our own power or holiness?

Jn 19:8–11 Jesus replied, "You would have no power over me at all if
it had not been given you from above."

Rom 11:33–36 Who has given anything to (the Lord) so that his presents
come only as a debt returned? Everything there is comes from
him . . .

Jer 23:23–24 Am I a God when near . . . and not a God when far away?
Do I not fill heaven and earth?

1 Cor 2:1–5 I came among you in weakness . . . and what I spoke . . .
was . . . to demonstrate the convincing power of the Spirit, so that
your faith should depend . . . on the power of God.

50. Witness

Lk 12:4–12 " . . . do not worry about . . . what to say, because when the time comes, the Holy Spirit will teach you what you should say."

Mt 5:13–16 "You are light for the world . . . your light must shine in people's sight, so that seeing your good works, they may give praise to your Father."

Jas 1:19–27 But you must do what the Word tells you and not just listen to it and deceive yourselves.

Phil 2:13–16 It is God who . . . gives you the intention and the powers to act . . . remain faultless and pure . . . like bright stars in the world, proffering to it the Word of life.

2 Tm 3:14–17 You must keep to what you have been taught and know to be true . . . remember . . . how . . . you have known the holy scriptures . . .

Phil 4:11–13 There is nothing I cannot do in the One who strengthens me.

2 Cor 10:3–6 . . . it is not by human methods that we do battle. . . . we bring every thought into . . . obedience to Christ.

1 Tm 4:7–16 . . . be an example to all . . . in the way you speak and behave . . . you have in you a spiritual gift.

Heb 6:10–11 God would not be so unjust as to forget all you have done, the love that you have for his name or the services you . . . are doing.

Mt 10:24–31 "It is enough for a disciple to grow to be like a teacher . . . so do not be afraid of them."

Suggestions for Further Reading

In any or all of the following books the reader will find nourishment for the inner desire of grace which may have led to interest in this present book.

Abhishiktananda, *Prayer*, Westminster, 1972.

Anonymous, *The Cloud of Unknowing* (trans. William Johnston), Doubleday Image Book, 1973.

Anthony Bloom, *Beginning To Pray*, Paulist Press, 1970.

———. *Living Prayer*, Templegate, 1966.

Leonard Boase, *The Prayer of Faith*, Loyola University Press (reprint), 1985.

James Borst, *Contemplative Prayer, A Guide for Today's Catholic*, Liguori, 1979.

James Finley, *The Awakening Call*, Ave Maria Press, 1986.

Willigis Jäger, *The Way to Contemplation*, Paulist Press, 1987.

William Johnston, *The Inner Eye of Love*, Harper & Row, 1982.

Thomas Keating, *Open Mind, Open Heart*, Amity House, 1986.

John Main, *Word into Silence*, Paulist Press, 1981.

Thomas Merton, *New Seeds of Contemplation*, New Directions, 1972.

———. *What Is Contemplation?* Templegate, 1981.

Table of Biblical Abbreviations

Acts—Acts of the Apostles
Am—Amos
Bar—Baruch
1 Chr—1 Chronicles
2 Chr—2 Chronicles
Col—Colossians
1 Cor—1 Corinthians
2 Cor—2 Corinthians
Dn—Daniel
Dt—Deuteronomy
Eccl—Ecclesiastes
Eph—Ephesians
Est—Esther
Ex—Exodus
Ez—Ezekiel
Ezr—Ezra
Gal—Galatians
Gn—Genesis
Hb—Habakkuk
Heb—Hebrews
Hg—Haggai
Hos—Hosea
Is—Isaiah
Jas—James
Jb—Job

Jdt—Judith
Jer—Jeremiah
Jgs—Judges
Jl—Joel
Jn—John
1 Jn—1 John
2 Jn—2 John
3 Jn—3 John
Jon—Jonah
Jos—Joshua
Jude—Jude
1 Kgs—1 Kings
2 Kgs—2 Kings
Lam—Lamentations
Lk—Luke
Lv—Leviticus
Mal—Malachi
1 Mc—1 Maccabees
2 Mc—2 Maccabees
Mi—Micah
Mk—Mark
Mt—Matthew
Na—Nahum
Neh—Nehemiah
Nm—Numbers

Ob—Obadiah
Phil—Philippians
Phlm—Philemon
Prv—Proverbs
Ps(s)—Psalms
1 Pt—1 Peter
2 Pt—2 Peter
Rom—Romans
Ru—Ruth
Rv—Revelation
Sir—Sirach
1 Sm—1 Samuel
2 Sm—2 Samuel
Song(Sg)—Song of Songs
Tb—Tobit
1 Thes—1 Thessalonians
2 Thes—2 Thessalonians
Ti—Titus
1 Tm—1 Timothy
2 Tm—2 Timothy
Wis—Wisdom
Zec—Zechariah
Zep—Zephaniah